Diagonal (or On-Point) Set

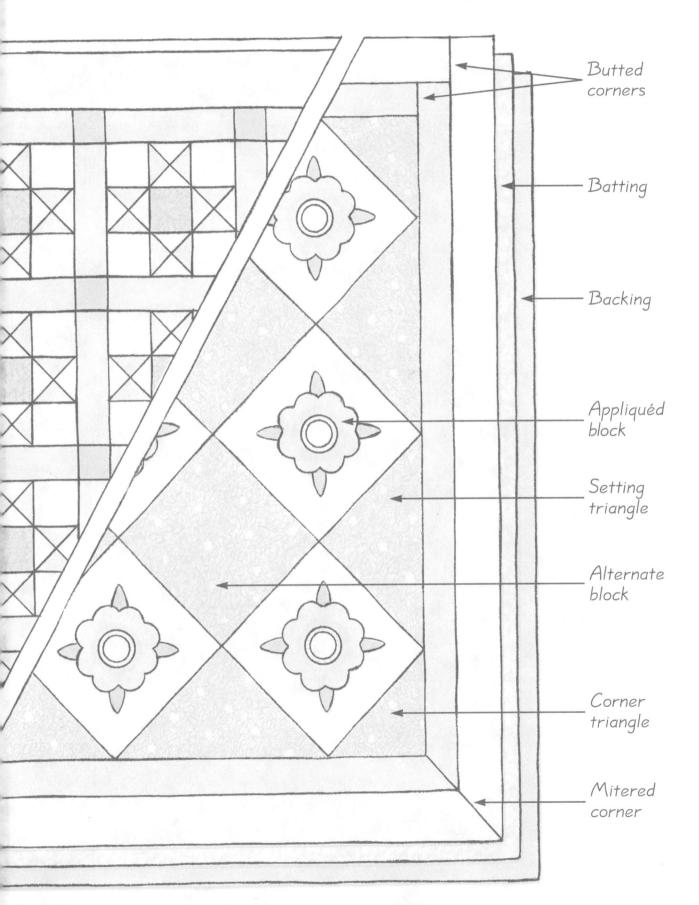

Butted corners

Batting

Backing

Appliquéd block

Setting triangle

Alternate block

Corner triangle

Mitered corner

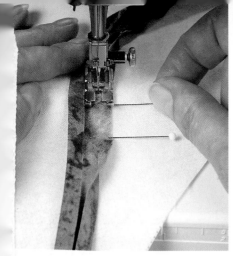
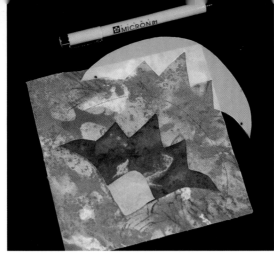

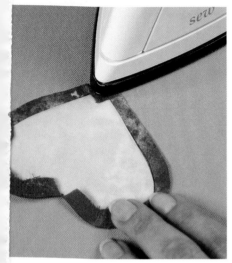
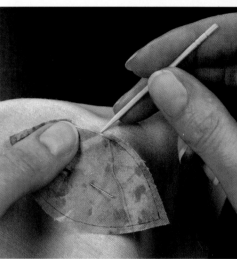

Rodale's Successful Quilting Library™

Appliqué Made Easy

Karen Costello Soltys
Editor

Rodale Press, Inc.
Emmaus, Pennsylvania

© 1998 by Rodale Press, Inc.

Editor: Karen Costello Soltys
Writers: Karen Kay Buckley, Mimi Dietrich,
 Cyndi Hershey, Jane Hill, Susan McKelvey,
 Jane Townswick, and Janet Wickell
Series Designer: Sue Gettlin
Design Coordinator and Cover Designer:
 Christopher Rhoads
Layout Designer: Keith Biery
Illustrator: Sandy Freeman
Photographer: John Hamel
Photo Direction and Stylist: Stan Green
Photography Editor: James A. Gallucci
Model: Anne Cassar
Copy Editor: Erana C. Bumbardatore
Manufacturing Coordinator: Patrick T. Smith
Indexer: Nan N. Badgett
Editorial Assistance: Jodi Guiducci and
 Sue Nickol

Rodale Home and Garden Books
Vice President and Editorial Director:
 Margaret J. Lydic
Managing Editor, Quilt Books:
 Suzanne Nelson
Director of Design and Production:
 Michael Ward
Associate Art Director: Carol Angstadt
Production Manager:
 Robert V. Anderson Jr.
Studio Manager: Leslie M. Keefe
Copy Director: Dolores Plikaitis
Book Manufacturing Manager:
 Mark Krahforst
Office Manager: Karen Earl-Braymer

We're always happy to hear from you.

For questions or comments concerning
the editorial content of this book,
please write to:

Rodale Press, Inc.
Book Readers' Service
33 East Minor Street
Emmaus, PA 18098

Look for other Rodale books wherever
books are sold. Or you may call us at
(800) 848–4735.

For more information about Rodale
Press and the books and magazines we
publish, visit our World Wide Web site:
http://www.rodalepress.com

Library of Congress Cataloging-in-Publication
Data published the first volume of this series as:

 Rodale's successful quilting library.
  p. cm.
 Includes index.
 ISBN 0–87596–760–4 (hc: v. 1:alk paper)
 1. Quilting. 2. Patchwork. I. Soltys, Karen
Costello. II. Rodale Press.
 TT835.R622 1997
 746.46'041—dc21 96–51316

Appliqué Made Easy:
 ISBN 0–87596–813–9

Distributed in the book trade
by St. Martin's Press

2 4 6 8 10 9 7 5 3 1 hardcover

Contents

Introduction

When the quilting bug first bit me, the word "appliqué" wasn't even in my vocabulary. I visualized making a patchwork quilt. And, of course, I assumed I would sew it entirely by machine. After all, the closest I had come to hand sewing was hemming skirts and sewing on buttons. So, you can imagine my surprise when my very first quilting instructor informed our class that we'd be making an appliqué block!

Well, a lot has changed, and I've appliquéd quite a lot in the last five years. Today I'm happy to say that I truly enjoy appliqué. Hand appliqué is a quiet and relaxing pastime, and it's one I can do in the family room rather than in my sewing room. I'm comforted knowing that I always have a hand appliqué project waiting to work on when I have a free evening.

What's more, I love machine appliqué, too. It's fun and exciting to see appliqué designs come to life quickly—and beautifully—under the needle of my machine. And with so many styles of machine appliqué to choose from, I can achieve many different looks, including the invisible type that fools just about everyone into thinking I stitched it by hand!

Whether you're just getting your feet wet with appliqué or you've been doing it for quite some time, you'll find lesson after lesson to make appliqué easier and more fun to do. We gathered some great appliqué artists, including Karen Kay

Buckley, Mimi Dietrich, Susan McKelvey, Janet Wickell, and Rodale's own Jane Townswick, to show you exactly what to do in every hand appliqué situation. From basic, gentle curves to the pointiest of points, they'll have you stitching like an expert in no time. If you're already familiar with the basics, you'll still love our tips from the pros, such as how to use a wooden toothpick and a glue stick to handle even the trickiest shapes. If you're quite experienced at appliqué, you'll enjoy learning about specialty techniques like reverse appliqué, cutwork appliqué, folk art appliqué, and dimensional appliqué.

When it comes to machine appliqué, we've got that covered, too. Cyndi Hershey, owner of The Country Quilt Shop in southeastern Pennsylvania, shares all her insider secrets—from getting shapes ready to appliqué to actually stitching them in place. And since she's a shop owner, she knows all about all the latest gadgets and products to make machine appliqué easier than ever. You'll see what they are and how to use them for successful results every time.

As a special bonus, we've asked Jane Hill to write about her special technique—making Molas by machine. This intricate design work traditionally involves dozens of hours of hand stitching. But Jane has simplified the whole process with fusible web and a sewing machine. If you're asking yourself, "What is a Mola, anyway?" now is your chance to find out! Or, if you've enjoyed Molas but didn't want to make one by hand, this chapter is for you.

One of the things I like most about appliqué is that there are so many ways to express your personal style. From exquisite Baltimore album–style appliqué to rustic folk art stitching, you can add as much elegance, whimsy, or charm as you like to your projects. You can use purchased patterns or create designs all your own. You can invest time in a one-of-a-kind needle-turn appliqué quilt, or you can make a quick and easy fusible appliqué project in an afternoon. There are no limitations on what you can create with appliqué.

So if you are like I was—resisting appliqué because you thought it could be successful only if you invested hours and hours—resist no more. Appliqué is creative, colorful, and most of all, rewarding. With this book in hand, you'll be able to accomplish any appliqué project you like. And, you can make those projects by hand or machine— the choice is yours. So, what are you waiting for? It's time to start a new appliqué project!

Karen Soltys

Karen Costello Soltys
Editor

20 Top Tips for *Appliqué*

1. There are many techniques for successful appliqué. If the first one you try doesn't feel comfortable, don't give up. Try them all, then use the techniques you like the best.

2. If your fusible web doesn't stick as well as it should, read the manufacturer's directions and make sure you're following them *exactly*. If you press longer than recommended, the glue will lose its adhesive quality.

3. It's hard to get all the edges on a curved shape to stick to the freezer paper. The wider your seam allowances, the harder it will be because there's more fabric to gather in to fit. Trim seam allowances along a curve down to ⅛ inch to reduce the bulk.

4. If you find the Quilter's GluTube messy to use, try these tips. To start, rub the GluTube on a scrap of paper until the roller ball tip gets the glue running smoothly. Then, don't overdo it. A thin line of glue is all you need. Finally, don't turn the fabric edges until the glue has had a little time to set up and become tacky so it won't seep out of the seam allowance.

5. Hand appliqué makes a nice take-along project. When traveling, you'll want to bring a large selection of thread colors without taking up a lot of space. Buy a plastic bobbin box, and fill it with bobbins wound with a variety of basic colors. You can leave the big spools at home.

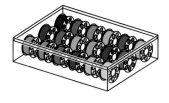

6. Fusible web makes quick work of appliqué, but it can make a project stiff to the touch. Reduce the stiffness by cutting out the full-size appliqué shape, then cutting away the center portion. Leave about ¼ inch of web for around the perimeter of your shapes. That's enough to secure them in place and keep them flexible.

7. If you like the iron-on quality of freezer paper but need to make many pieces of the same shape, first make a plastic template. It's a lot easier to trace around the plastic template onto freezer paper than it is to repeatedly trace over a printed pattern.

8. Resealable plastic bags are great storage and carrying cases for appliqué projects. They keep everything neatly together, and since they're see-through, you'll know at a glance what's in them.

9. When using a purchased appliqué pattern (one that's not printed in a book), you can eliminate the tracing step. Stick clear Con-Tact paper over the printed pattern pieces and cut them out. The shapes are durable and firm enough to trace around.

10. To remove freezer paper from underneath finished appliqués, you need to cut the background fabric. You can cut away the entire background (leaving ¼ inch for seam allowances). But if you prefer to leave the background intact, make a diagonal snip. The bias cut won't fray.

11. Also, *never* stitch closed the opening that you cut to remove freezer paper. It will create a ridge that will show through on the front of your quilt. Just smooth the cut with your fingertip and leave it. Once the quilt's layered and

quilted, no one will ever know that there are slits under your appliqués.

12 Get organized so you can spend more time appliquéing than looking for what you need. Try the Worm Book (found in fishing supply stores), which has zippered plastic "pages" inside a three-ring binder, or the appliqué project totes from Quilt A'bout or TRS, which have zippered sections that are perfect for keeping a portable project organized.

13 Here's an easy way to handle thread tails when machine satin stitching. Insert the needle and turn the flywheel to bring up the needle. Tug on the top thread to pull the bobbin thread to the surface. Hold the thread tails in front, in line with the edge of the appliqué, and zigzag over them. After a few stitches, you can snip them off and they'll

be completely covered by the satin stitch.

14 If you find it difficult to take the tiny hand stitches necessary to hold a seam allowance under, particularly on the second side of inside and outside points, try sewing in regular length stitches out to about ¼ inch past the point. Then turn the appliqué and stitch back in the opposite direction. Space your stitches so that they fall between the previous ones.

15 In hand appliqué, you can stitch either along the top edge or the bottom edge. Many appliquérs prefer the top edge, where they are looking over the folded edge or the "mountain." Others prefer stitching along the bottom edge, or the "valley," where they can see the exact edge of the fold. If hand appliqué is new to you, try both ways to see which is more comfortable for you.

16 If your thread tangles hopelessly around silk pins as you stitch, give ¾-inch sequin pins a try! Put them in from the *wrong* side of your work, and suddenly appliqué will be a breeze.

17 When facing appliqués for machine stitching, trim away the excess inter-

facing and appliqué fabric with pinking shears. The jagged edge reduces bulk and prevents a ridge from showing through the final appliqué.

18 Whenever you are hand stitching, change your needle often so that you always have a fine, sharp point.

19 If your invisible thread breaks often, take it off of the machine and place it in a jar or box on the floor. The spool can bounce around in its confined space, and the thread can then feed easily off the spool. Bring the thread up through a paper clip or safety pin taped to the right rear corner at the top of the machine, and proceed to thread the machine as usual.

20 A too-hot iron is usually at fault when freezer paper templates won't separate cleanly. To avoid this "sticky" problem, use a *dry* iron on a *medium* setting for freezer paper templates. Press just long enough for the paper to adhere—no more than a second or two. If removal is still a problem, use tweezers to extract the paper, and spritz lightly with cool water to remove waxy residue.

Everything You Need
for Machine Appliqué

Do you love the look of appliqué but find yourself short on time? Or maybe hand stitching is not your favorite pastime? Machine appliqué could be just the answer for you! There are many different methods from which to choose, each with a different look. From an elaborate heirloom Baltimore album quilt with virtually invisible stitches to a primitive wool project using blanket stitches and heavy cotton thread, the world of appliqué by machine is fun and easy to master.

Getting Ready

An open-toe presser foot for your machine is a basic requirement. This type of foot, which is cut back to *behind* the needle, gives you a clear view of what and where you are stitching. You can get one from your machine dealer, or look for generic feet that correspond to the shank type of your machine at quilt shops.

You will need other supplies depending on which method of machine appliqué you choose. Many of them are described in this chapter. Specific directions for how to use specialty products can be found in the next chapter, "Preparing Shapes for Machine Appliqué."

Top thread: cotton, rayon, or metallic

Bobbin thread: Bobbinfil or 60 wt. machine embroidery

Appropriate size and type of machine needle

Stabilizer

Paper-backed fusible appliqué web or water-soluble glue stick

Template plastic

Freezer paper

Thread snips or embroidery scissors

Sewing machine

Open-toe presser foot

Basic Supplies for Machine Appliqué

Cotton Threads

Cotton thread is suitable for all stitch methods except for mock hand appliqué. Consider the thread weight as it relates to your specific appliqué project.

• 40 wt. (machine quilting thread): Great for buttonhole stitch method, especially when stitching on heavier fabrics such as homespun, flannel, corduroy, or wool.
• 50 wt. (silk finish or long fiber types): A good all-purpose thread suitable for almost every stitch method. The longer fibers help prevent a "fuzzy" look.
• 60 wt. (machine embroidery thread): Excellent for appliquéing lighter-weight fabrics and small-scale pieces or for using when you simply want as delicate a look as possible.

Experiment with the color of your thread. Try contrasting the thread against the appliqué instead of matching it for a slightly different look.

Decorative Threads

Rayon thread commonly comes in 30 wt. and 40 wt.; 30 wt. is slightly heavier. Rayon lends a wonderful sheen to a project and comes in a wide array of solid and variegated colors.

Metallic thread comes in two basic types: core wrapped or flat ("sliver"). They can add a touch of sparkle to a project but are not as durable as other threads. Metallic thread works well for straight-stitch appliqué and can also be used in satin or button-hole stitching.

Rayon   Metallic

Nylon & Bobbinfil

Tip

Since the bobbin thread won't be seen, the color is not critical. There's no need to change it to match your top thread.

Superfine nylon thread is soft and delicate and will be nearly invisible against your fabrics, making it a perfect choice for mock hand appliqué. Be sure to use size 0.004 or finer to achieve the best result, and choose a quality brand such as YLI or Sulky.

There are basically two types of thread recommended for the bobbin: 60 wt. cotton embroidery and Bobbinfil. They are both lightweight threads and may be used with any of the top threads mentioned above.

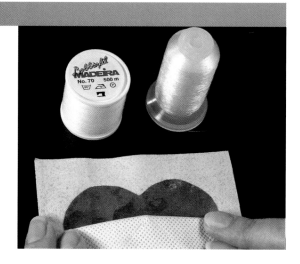

Sharp or Universal Needles

Choosing the right size and type of needle is very important for machine appliqué. The eye, shank, and taper of a needle all have an effect on the quality of your stitching. **Sharp or universal needles are basic sewing needles, and they're the best choices when working with cotton thread or nylon.**

• 60/8. Use with 60 wt. embroidery or nylon thread on broadcloth-weight cotton or finer fabrics.
• 70/10. Use with 50 wt. cotton or nylon thread on most cottons.
• 80/12. Use with 50 wt. cotton or nylon thread when stitching on slightly heavier fabrics. Also use with 40 wt. cotton thread.
• 90/14. Use with 40 or 50 wt. cotton threads on heavier fabrics.

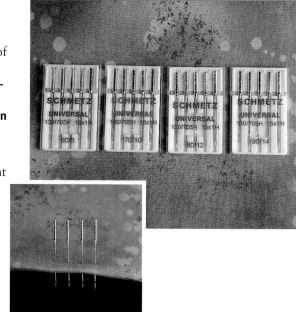

Embroidery & Metallic Needles

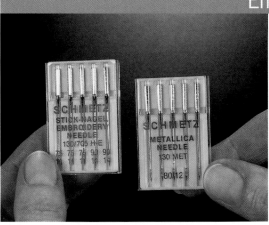

Embroidery needles are perfect for stitching with rayon thread. They protect the thread and prevent the shredding and breakage that may occur when using another type of needle.

• 75/11. Use with 40 wt. rayon thread on broadcloth-weight cotton.
• 90/14. Use with 40 wt. rayon thread on heavier fabric, or with 30 wt. rayon thread.

Metallica and Metalfil needles are the best choice for metallic threads.

• 80/12. Works well with most metallic threads and fabrics.

Stabilizers

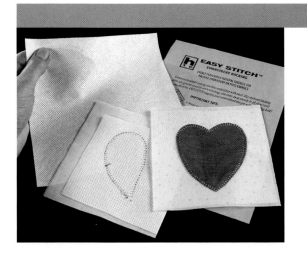

Placing a stabilizer between the fabric and the feed dogs of your machine helps prevent the background fabric from shifting, and it gives you more control when stitching. **A stabilizer also helps ensure that the stitches look nice and even, with no skips or knots.** A basic perforated stabilizer, such as Easy Tear, is all that most machine appliqué projects need. This type of stabilizer is slightly cushioned, which helps it to grip the feed dogs and gives you good control.

Tip

Avoid using paper or freezer paper as a stabilizer for appliqué. It gives minimal control, and it's hard to remove from zigzag stitches.

Fusible Webs & Interfacings

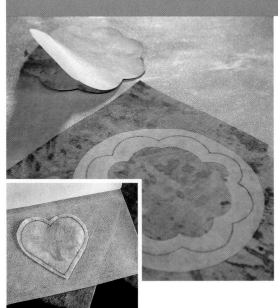

For satin or buttonhole stitch, you can "anchor" appliqué shapes to the background with fusible web. Like a stabilizer, it gives you better control when stitching. And since the appliqué edges aren't turned under, the adhesive helps prevent edges from fraying between the stitches. Many types of fusible products are available. Heat n Bond Light, Wonder Under, and Aleen's Hot Stitch are all suitable.

An alternative to fusible web is fusible interfacing. It's used to face appliqué shapes so raw edges will be neatly turned under. Faced shapes are fused to the background for stitching. See "Preparing Shapes for Machine Appliqué" on page 16 for details.

EVERYTHING FOR MACHINE APPLIQUÉ

Glue Sticks & GluTube

When you're working with small appliqué pieces or when it's not critical that the entire shape be held down, a glue stick is suitable. Glue sticks come in both permanent and temporary types. Be sure to look for a water-soluble product for appliqué.

Quilter's GluTube is a rubber cement product that stays soft and flexible. This glue is not water-soluble, but when applied correctly (see page 19), it won't affect your sewing machine needle. This product lends itself well to mock hand appliqué, where you're using freezer paper as a template.

Template Plastic

Clear template plastic is readily available and easy to work with. You can see through the plastic for easy tracing of the original appliqué pattern, and then cut out the shapes with craft scissors. Simply trace around the plastic templates with a pencil or Pigma pen on the right side of the fabric.

Templar, a heat-resistant template product, is also available. It looks similar to plastic template sheets; however, Templar is actually made of nylon. You can use Templar as a guide for pressing over seam allowances on appliqué pieces since it can withstand the heat of an iron. See page 74 for more details.

Freezer Paper

Freezer paper (American-style) can also be used to make templates. The advantage is that you can cut out the shapes easily and then press them to your fabric. Since the paper adheres to your fabric, the template doesn't shift as you cut or trace the shapes. A disadvantage is that paper edges don't hold up as long as plastic ones, so a freezer paper template cannot be reused more than once or twice.

Freezer paper is available in grocery stores as well as in many quilt shops.

The Quilter's
Problem Solver

Finding the Right Supplies

Problem	Solution
Nearest quilt shop doesn't carry many appliqué supplies.	If you don't live near a quilt shop and need to rely on mail-order or chain store shopping for your needs, here are a few mail-order sources that carry various recommended products: **Nancy's Notions**—needles, dozens of threads, open-toe appliqué feet, fusible webs, stabilizers, fabrics, and more. (800) 833–0690. **The Quilt Farm**—needles, threads, Quilter's GluTube, freezer paper, fusible web, fabrics, and more. (800) 435–6201. **Keepsake Quilting**—threads, Quilters' GluTube, freezer paper, fusible web, fabrics, and more. (800) 865–9458. **Web of Thread**—every thread imaginable, needles, and more. (800) 955–8185.

Skill Builder

Beautiful machine appliqué starts with the right tools and supplies for the job.

❏ Buy ¼ yard of several types of fusible web products to experiment with—then use the one that gives *you* the best results.

❏ If you don't want the added weight or stiffness of a fusible product in your quilt, use freezer paper or a tear-away stabilizer instead. They stabilize your shapes as you stitch but are removed from the quilt.

❏ Keep a supply of machine needles on hand so you'll always have the right type and size ready to go when you are. Sometimes it takes a bit of experimenting with thread and needle combinations to get just the right one for your machine and project.

Try This!

Experiment with threads for unusual effects. If you like the look and texture of folk art appliqué, don't limit your thread choices to the basics. If you appliqué wool, felt, or flannel shapes, try a textured thread, too. Burmilana is one type of woolly thread that comes in many colors and can help you carry out the rustic look. However, you will definitely have to change your needle for this thread. To get the bulk of the thread through the fabric layers, switch to a jeans needle, size 90/14.

EVERYTHING FOR MACHINE APPLIQUÉ

15

Preparing Shapes for
Machine Appliqué

You've gathered all of your appliqué supplies, and you're ready to start! But before you can actually sew, you need to prepare your appliqué shapes. You won't want to skimp on this stage. The more care you take to get your shapes ready for stitching, the better looking your finished project will be.

Getting Ready

You'll need to decide what type of appliqué stitching you want to do because different methods require different preparation.

Mock hand appliqué and straight stitch appliqué require *prepared edge* shapes. This means the seam allowance is folded under on each piece before stitching. There are several ways to do this, and these same techniques can be used for hand appliqué. The goal is to get the edges as smooth as possible, without any jagged points.

Satin stitch and blanket stitch (sometimes referred to as buttonhole stitch) appliqué require *raw edge* treatment. Since both of these methods seal the edges of the fabric shapes, you do not need to turn or roll under the edges. Shapes are usually attached to the background fabric with fusible web or glue stick before stitching.

See "The Stitch Sampler" on page 32 for help deciding which type of machine stitching you want to do.

See "The Stitch Sampler" on page 32

What You'll Need

- **Featherweight nonfusible interfacing**
- **Fabric markers: chalk, pencils, or Pigma pens**
- **Silk or appliqué pins**
- **Sewing machine**
- **Embroidery scissors**
- **Iron and ironing board**
- **Featherweight fusible interfacing**
- **Freezer paper**
- **Paper or craft scissors**
- **Fabric scissors**
- **Quilters' GluTube**
- **Water-soluble glue stick**
- **Lightweight fusible web**

Faced Appliqué

Using a facing for appliqué shapes makes it quite easy to have perfectly turned-under edges. The facing edge makes the turn-under guideline, and the facing fabric holds the edges in place. There's no chance of edges rolling out or fraying.

Place featherweight *nonfusible* interfacing over your appliqué pattern. **Trace the designs with a pencil or Pigma pen.** Cut out the shapes, leaving a scant ¼-inch seam allowance around the drawn lines. **Place the shapes on the *right* side of your selected fabric, and pin them in place.**

SHAPES FOR MACHINE APPLIQUÉ

1

17

2

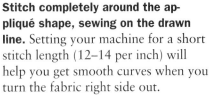

Stitch completely around the appliqué shape, sewing on the drawn line. Setting your machine for a short stitch length (12–14 per inch) will help you get smooth curves when you turn the fabric right side out.

Cut out fabric even with the interfacing. **Insert the sharp tip of embroidery scissors into the interfacing and make a short slit across the middle.** Clip curves and V-shaped inner points. At any outside points, blunt trim the seam allowance to remove the point and reduce bulk. Now turn the appliqué through the slit. Press the faced appliqué flat.

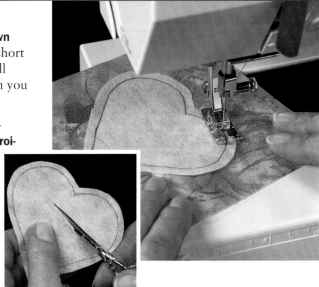

3

Featherweight *fusible* interfacing offers an alternative to nonfusible interfacing. When you sew the fusible interfacing and fabric together, however, be sure that the right side of the fabric and the *fusible side* of the interfacing (it usually has telltale little dots) are against each other. After stitching, slice and turn as described in Step 2. **The fusible side will be facing out, allowing you to fuse the appliqué to the background fabric.**

Finger press the shape rather than using an iron, or your appliqué will stick to the ironing board!

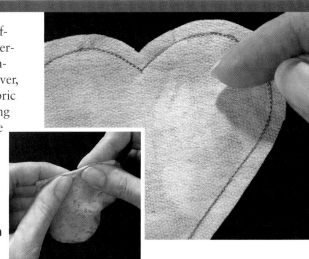

Freezer Paper Appliqué

1

To use freezer paper as a guide for turning under edges, place it over the appliqué pattern—paper side up, shiny side down. Trace the design, then cut it out on the drawn lines. **Pin the template on the wrong side of the fabric, shiny side facing out, and cut out the piece with a scant ¼-inch seam allowance. Using the tip of a hot, dry iron, push the seam allowance over the edge of the paper. The fabric will adhere to the paper.** Leave the paper in the shape for stitching.

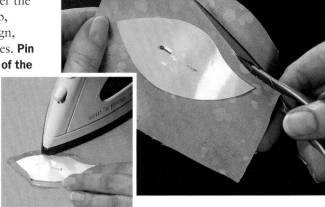

Tip

Use pinking shears to cut out the shapes. It reduces bulk and prevents a ridge from showing where the seam allowances are turned in.

Tip

Use a knitting needle or chopstick to push out the edges and make them smooth when turning fabric, since you can't use an iron.

Tip

Clip into any Vs and around any curves before pressing for smoother curves and pointier points.

Another way to use the holding power of freezer paper is to trace the appliqué pattern as in Step 1. Then, instead of pinning the shape on top of your fabric, press the freezer paper template to the *wrong* side of your fabric. Remember to have the shiny side down! **Now cut out the fabric, adding a scant ¼-inch seam allowance.** To turn under the edges, follow Step 3.

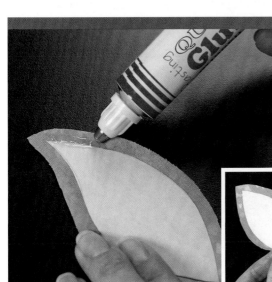

3

Using Quilters' GluTube, apply a light but continuous layer of glue to the edge of the template and the fabric seam allowance. Allow the glue to dry for a few seconds, then roll the seam over the edge of the paper. **Use your fingers to smooth edges as you go.** Important: Do not iron these edges. If you need to adjust, you can easily peel and reposition the fabric as necessary.

You can use this same method using a temporary hold glue stick (such as Post-it brand) instead of the Quilters' GluTube.

Glue Stick

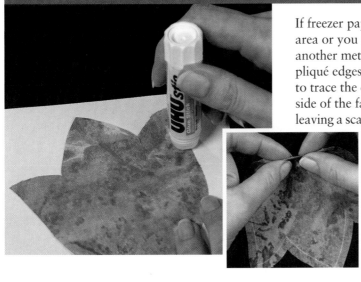

If freezer paper is hard to find in your area or you prefer not to use it, here's another method for turning under appliqué edges. Use a #2 pencil or chalk to trace the design *lightly* on the *right* side of the fabric. Cut out the shape leaving a scant ¼-inch seam allowance. **Using a water-soluble glue stick, dab glue around the seam allowance edges on the *wrong* side of the fabric. Fold the seam allowance over exactly on the marked lines and pinch the edges together.**

SHAPES FOR MACHINE APPLIQUÉ

Raw Edge Preparation

1

Fusible web not only lets you permanently adhere your appliqué shapes to the background for easy stitching, it tames the raw edges of your shapes and helps prevent fraying. Trace the appliqué design onto the paper side of a lightweight fusible web. Note: The finished design will be the reverse image of what you originally trace. If this affects your design, trace the design in reverse to start with.

Cut the design from the web, cutting *outside* the drawn lines. Do not cut exactly on the lines.

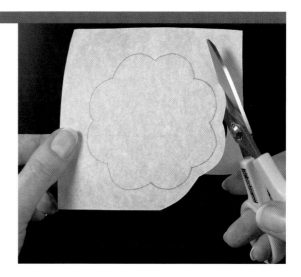

2

Follow the product instructions for fusing to the wrong side of the fabric. When cool, cut out the appliqué exactly on the drawn lines. **Peel away the paper backing.** Arrange the appliqués onto the background in the correct order, and fuse them into place. See page 22 for more information on layering shapes in order.

3

The above method for fusible web works great for small appliqué shapes. However, if your pieces are larger than a half-dollar or will be layered, you may not want the extra body that fusible web adds to your project. To reduce the stiffness, trace and cut out the shape from fusible web, as described in Step 1. **Before you fuse to fabric, cut out the web shape again approximately ¼ inch *inside* the drawn lines, leaving only a rim of the fusible web. Now fuse to the fabric and cut out the final shape as in Step 2.**

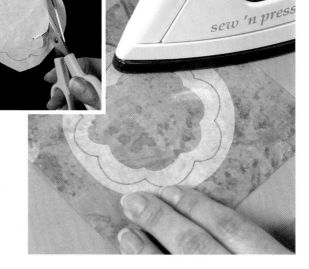

The Quilter's
Problem Solver

Taming Tricky Edges

Problem	Solution
When pressing points with a freezer paper template, points don't turn out as sharp as they should.	First, press the point of fabric up and over the point of the template. Then, push in the sides of the seam allowance against the edge of the freezer paper with the tip of the iron. Use the tip of a pin or embroidery scissors to hold the point in place while you press the sides.
Threads fray around edges where seam allowance was clipped for ease.	To prevent fraying, use small, sharp embroidery scissors for the most control when clipping. Clip only three-quarters of the depth of the seam allowance, not all the way to the turn-under line. You'll still have plenty of ease in the fabric. To fix a piece that's already frayed, swipe a wooden toothpick across the top of your glue stick. Then pass the toothpick over the frayed threads to push them back in place. This tiny amount of glue will do the trick.

Skill Builder

Experiment with all of the methods to find out what works best for you. Here are a few additional tips to improve your results.

❏ Use a wooden bread cutting board (preferably a new one) when preparing shapes with freezer paper. Pressing against a hard surface instead of an ironing board gives you crisper edges.

❏ Tape the pattern to a window or onto a light box with the *wrong side up*. With the light shining through, you should be able to clearly see the pattern lines. Tape the web over the pattern and trace.

❏ Use a heart to try each technique. It's the perfect shape because it has curves and straight lines, as well as inner and outer points. Plus it's easy to draw or cut from paper.

Try This!

Fusible fleece is an easy way to add dimension to your appliqué shapes. If you're using a prepared edge technique, fuse a finished size appliqué shape of fusible fleece to the wrong side of the fabric before sewing or pressing over the seam allowances. With fusible web, fuse fleece to the wrong side of fabric before fusing web onto it, then continue as usual. It's like instant trapunto!

Placing & Layering
Appliqué Shapes

One of the trickier parts of appliqué is knowing how to layer the pieces that need to overlap and how to place them accurately on the background fabric for stitching. Internationally known teacher Mimi Dietrich shares two techniques that make it easy to position and layer shapes. You can mark designs directly on your background fabric, or you can use a plastic overlay to ensure that the appliqué pieces are placed accurately. These techniques apply to both hand and machine appliqué and will help you sew your appliqués in place perfectly.

Getting Ready

Choose a background fabric appropriate for your appliqué design. Solid, light fabrics or tone-on-tone prints will highlight the appliqué pieces, however, today anything goes! Plaids, prints, darks, and brights can all make effective background fabrics, depending on the look you're after. Prewash and press your background fabric so that it will look neat and crisp.

A large square ruler will help you mark and cut all of your appliqué background squares accurately. A light box is a great tool to help you trace the designs.

Also, you can prepare your appliqué shapes—either for hand or machine appliqué. Whatever method you choose, the ideas presented here for layering the shapes will apply.

Marking Appliqué Placement

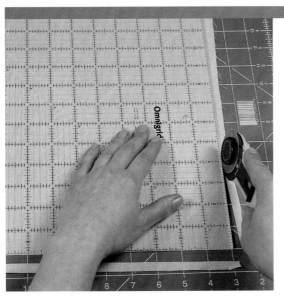

1

Cut the background fabric larger than the pattern calls for, adding 1 inch to each side of the background square when you cut it out. For instance, if you need a 10-inch finished square, add ½ inch for seam allowances, plus 1 inch on all sides for a 12½-inch square. You can trim it to the correct size when the appliqué is complete.

Place the corner of the square ruler with the 1-inch marks (as opposed to the 12-inch or 15-inch markings) in the corner of your fabric. Cut along the two adjacent sides of the ruler past the measurement of the size of your square.

Tip

It's best to cut the background fabric oversize because appliqué sometimes causes ripples in the fabric or frays along the outer edges.

PLACING & LAYERING APPLIQUÉ SHAPES

23

2

Tip

If your fabric is loosely woven, don't pick it up to turn it. Simply turn the mat instead.

Turn the fabric around and place the ruler on the fabric so the dimensions you need (12½ inches in this case) are aligned with the cut edges. Cut along both edges of the ruler to create a perfect square.

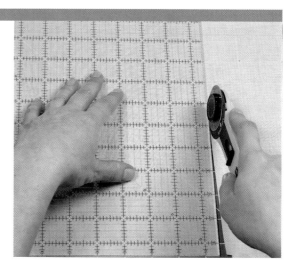

3

If your pattern doesn't have the center marked, **use a ruler to measure the pattern and mark the center both vertically and horizontally.**

Tape your pattern to the table or light box so that it will not slip. Scotch Removable Magic Tape will not rip the paper when you pull it up later.

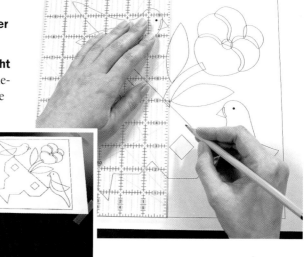

4

Find the center of the background fabric by folding the square in half, then folding it into quarters. Match the cut ends carefully. Finger press the folds to mark placement guidelines for your appliqué pieces. It might be tempting to press the creases with an iron so they're easier to see, but try to resist this urge. Pressed-in creases will be hard to get out later.

Place the center fold of the fabric over the center mark on your pattern. Gently unfold the fabric, keeping the center folds aligned with the center marks. **Tape the fabric securely over the paper pattern.**

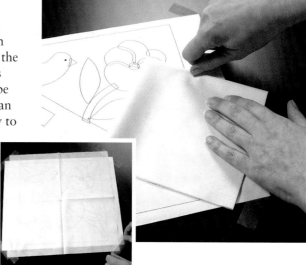

Trace the design *lightly* onto your background fabric. These guidelines help you place the appliqué pieces accurately on the background fabric. Trace all of the shapes exactly on the lines. Some quilters like to trace with dotted lines. Use a silver pencil or a mechanical pencil. Use a white chalk pencil for dark fabrics.

If you're tracing over a light box, it's easy to trace too darkly without realizing it. Make a sample to test your tracing.

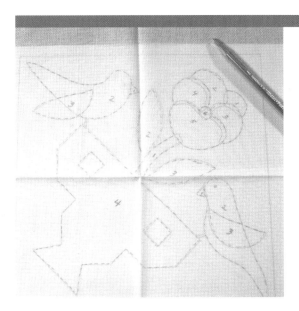

If your pattern has numbers referring to stitching sequence, transfer the numbers to the background fabric. If there are no numbers, think about the order in which you will stitch the appliqué pieces. For example, floral designs are usually stitched in this order: stems, leaves, flowers. Assign your own numbers to make keeping track of the stitching order simple.

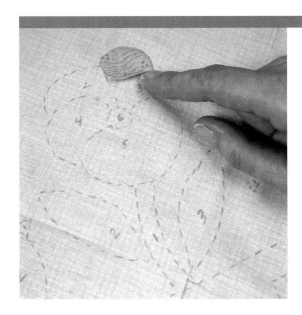

When appliqué pieces overlap, it is called layered appliqué. It is important that the underneath pieces are stitched in place first. Other pieces will overlap or layer over the previous piece.

When you appliqué the first piece, do not turn under seam allowances that will be covered by other appliqué pieces. They should lie flat under the top piece. This technique is much easier than trying to butt or match the pieces like puzzle pieces.

PLACING & LAYERING APPLIQUÉ SHAPES

8

When you are layering one piece completely on top of another piece, you will cover the placement guidelines with the first piece. Make a "window" to guide your layering. On a piece of paper, trace the design. Cut out the large design (flower) around the outside edge. Then cut out the inner design (flower center). **Place the window over the flower, then drop the flower center through the window for perfect placement.** Pin and stitch as usual.

9

Tip

Use a permanent marking pen to trace onto the acetate. It won't smear off.

One of the downfalls of marking the design on the background fabric is that your prepared shapes may not perfectly cover all your marks. If you do not want to mark your background fabric (or if it is dark and you cannot mark it), you may want to try a plastic or vinyl overlay for placing your appliqué pieces. Trace or photocopy the design onto a sheet of clear acetate. **Center the plastic sheet over the background fabric. Gently lift the plastic sheet, and slip an appliqué piece under the plastic.**

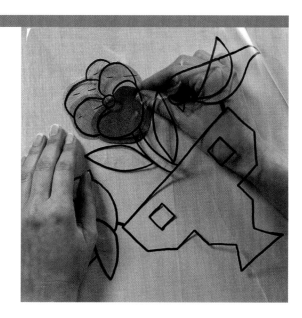

10

Tip

To keep glue sticks from drying out, store them in the refrigerator when they're not in use.

Unless the shapes are prepared with fusible web, you'll need to baste them in place. **Baste the pieces onto the background fabric in the order that they are numbered.** Pin-baste the pieces using small ¾-inch-long appliqué pins. Some quilters use a water-soluble glue stick to quickly and easily attach the pieces to the background. Others use thread to baste the pieces in place. Thread basting takes longer and it has to be removed later, but it helps avoid snagging your thread on pins as you appliqué.

The Quilter's
Problem Solver

Placing Shapes with Accuracy

Problem	Solution
Can't see through off-white fabric to trace the appliqué design.	If you're not using a light box, it can be hard to see the design, especially if it's taped to a dark table. Slip a piece of plain white paper under your pattern. It will make the lines clearer.
Can't see through dark background fabric to trace the appliqué design.	Place the pattern and fabric on a light box. The light will shine through, and you will be able to see the design. If necessary, trace over the design on the paper pattern with a dark marker. Or use the acetate method described in Step 9 on the opposite page.
Appliqué pieces slip when pinned to the background fabric.	Place your background fabric over a well-stuffed pillow. Position the pieces and stick pins through the pieces, straight down into the pillow. Gently lift the background fabric, then turn the pins to secure the fabric in place.

Skill Builder

Use these additional tips when preparing your background fabric.

❏ If you're a novice with a rotary cutter, use a square rotary-cutting ruler to mark your square, then cut it out carefully with scissors. Always *cut* the fabric; don't tear it.

❏ Test your fabric marker to make sure that it will wash out of the background fabric. Write your name on a small scrap of background fabric and wash it. If the marks come out, your marker is safe. If you cannot find a marker that will wash out, trace the pattern design slightly inside the design lines so that the marks will be completely covered by the appliqué pieces.

Try This!

If you do not have a light box, make your own. Open your dining room table and place a storm window over the opening. Put a lamp on the floor and let the light shine up through the glass to create your own light box!

Another creative solution is to put a light (an Ott Light works great) under a Plexiglas sewing table or even under a glass casserole dish.

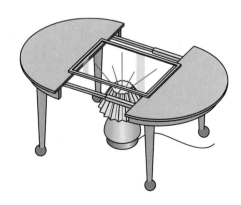

Unit Appliqué by
Hand & Machine

Layering shapes creates beautiful dimension in your appliqué—in everything from flowers to landscapes. Sometimes it is easier to sew (or fuse) various parts of an appliqué motif together before attaching them to the background fabric. Rather than stitching the bottom piece of the appliqué to the background and working up to the top piece, you can work in the opposite direction. Appliqué the topmost piece onto the fabric below it, and so on, until you've completed the motif you're working on. It's easy to maneuver the fabrics so you have better control. When the unit is complete, you simply stitch it onto the background.

Getting Ready

Investigate your appliqué pattern before you decide how to stitch it. Are there shapes that are layered or overlapped that could be appliquéd together before you stitch them to the background? Or is the pattern fairly basic, with most motifs being a single layer? If you find that you're working with complex flowers or other layered motifs, you may want to switch the order of stitching from bottom to top and try top-to-bottom unit appliqué.

For hand appliqué, you'll still need to make templates for each shape (either freezer paper or plastic—see page 66 for details), but don't trace them all onto fabric.

A variation of this technique works for fusible appliqués that you plan to finish with machine stitching. Prepare your individual shapes as described on pages 17–20. But don't fuse anything to the background until you've read this lesson!

Unit Appliqué by Hand

1

When you make your templates for appliqué pieces, mark the points on them where the adjacent pieces intersect or overlap. These markings will be used as guidelines for matching your pieces to form the unit. Select the fabric for the top section of the appliqué unit, and prepare the fabric for your favorite method of appliqué.

Transfer the intersection markings to the appliqué in the seam allowance.

2

Pin or baste the shape to a square of fabric that is large enough to accommodate the shape for the next layer of appliqué. If the pieces are only to be overlapped, not one completely on top of the other, simply overlap the fabrics as you baste. But make sure you leave enough room on the background for both the underneath appliqué shape plus a seam allowance. **An acetate or vinyl tracing of the complete unit laid over the pieces will guarantee that your placement will work.**

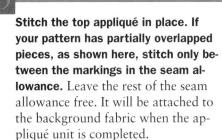

 Tip

See page 26 for information on making and using a vinyl or acetate overlay.

3

Stitch the top appliqué in place. If your pattern has partially overlapped pieces, as shown here, stitch only between the markings in the seam allowance. Leave the rest of the seam allowance free. It will be attached to the background fabric when the appliqué unit is completed.

4

Tip

If there are more than two layers to the unit, remember to mark intersection lines where the second and third layers meet.

When stitching is complete, lay the template for piece two over the partial unit, aligning it with the top appliqué piece where they are to butt. If your template is plastic, trace around the template to create a turn-under line for needle turning the second appliqué. If you are using freezer paper, press the template in place. **When marking is complete, cut out the shape a scant ¼ inch from the marked line or freezer paper edge.**

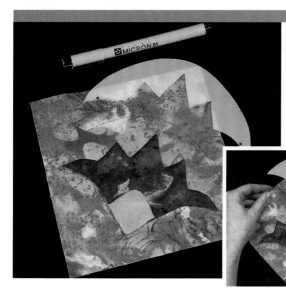

Appliqué the partial unit to the next layer, following the same process as for layer two. Continue in this manner until the entire unit is complete. If you are using needle-turn appliqué, you can proceed and appliqué the unit onto the background. **If you prefer freezer paper appliqué, make a freezer paper template the size of the entire unit by tracing the original pattern.** Press the paper onto the fabric and proceed as with any other single-layer appliqué.

Fusible Unit Appliqué

For machine appliqué it is difficult to use unit appliqué when shapes are prepared with freezer paper or facings because the layers are thick and removing the freezer paper is difficult. However, for fusible appliqué, you can prepare an entire multipieced unit before pressing it onto the background.

Prepare each shape in the unit with fusible web on the back and cut them out. **Using a Teflon pressing sheet on your ironing board, layer the pieces in the unit from bottom to top.**

Tip

Tweezers are very helpful in arranging pieces. They let you pick up and place tiny pieces without disturbing the other pieces.

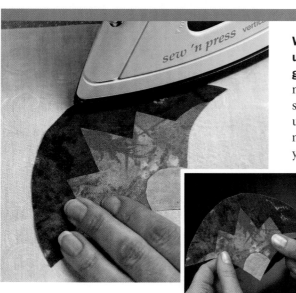

When everything is placed correctly, use the iron to press the pieces together. The fusible web will stick the multiple pieces together, but it won't stick to the Teflon pressing sheet. By using a pressing sheet, if you make a mistake in pressing the unit together, you simply start the unit over—not the entire block!

Peel the unit off of the pressing sheet and place it on the background fabric as desired. Press it in place, and you are ready for stitching. You can either stitch around each individual shape, or simply stitch around the perimeter of the unit.

Tip

If you stitch around each shape, stitch pieces in the same order as you layered them—bottom to top. That way, starting and stopping points will be concealed.

The Stitch
Sampler

Y ou can turn the variety of stitches and threads available into many different looks for machine appliqué projects. Many newer sewing machines have an assortment of both functional and decorative stitches that will expand your design possibilities. However, if you have a machine with limited stitch selection, you will still be able to do beautiful and imaginative machine appliqué simply by trying different threads. It's time to get creative!

Getting Ready

Look over your selected appliqué pattern and decide which stitching method will give you the effect you want. Do you want the look of traditional appliqué? If so, a mock hand or very fine satin stitch works well because the stitching does not detract from the overall design on the quilt. Are you making a primitive or folk art style project? The blanket or feather stitch method will probably give you just the look you want.

Before making your final decision, you also need to consider how the item will be used. Durability is an important consideration if you're appliquéing onto a garment, so consider satin, straight, or blanket stitch, as they completely seal the edges of the appliqué shapes. Mock hand appliqué is more delicate and would not be appropriate for a project that will receive a lot of wear.

See "Everything You Need for Machine Appliqué" on page 10 to select needles and threads as well as "Preparing Shapes for Machine Appliqué" on page 16.

See "Everything You Need for Machine Appliqué" on page 10 to select needles and threads as well as "Preparing Shapes for Machine Appliqué" on page 16.

What You'll Need

Sewing machine

Open-toe presser foot

Appropriate size and type of needles

Top thread: cotton, rayon, invisible nylon, or metallic

Bobbin thread: Bobbinfil or 60 wt. cotton embroidery

Thread snips or embroidery scissors

Appliqué fabrics

Stabilizer

Sampling the Stitches

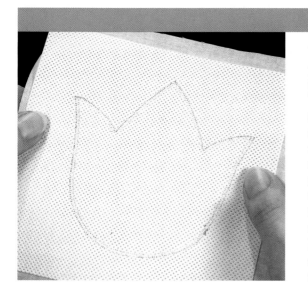

Adjusting Tension

Whatever machine appliqué stitch you use, you never want the bobbin thread to show on top of the design. To ensure that the bobbin thread stays underneath your work, you may need to loosen the top tension so the top thread will be pulled slightly to the underside of the work. **When you view the stitching from the wrong side, you should see a slight line of the top thread on either side of the bobbin thread.** Increasing the bobbin tension may also be necessary, but try working with just the top tension first.

To adjust your tension, either top thread or bobbin, remember: "righty tighty, lefty loosey."

33

Starting & Stopping

Since most stitches used are not simple straight stitches, making a machine knot by stitching up and down in the same place is not an option. **Take a few stitches, stop and pull up the bobbin thread to clip it off even with the surface of the fabric.** Overlap beginning stitches slightly with the ending stitches. Clip the thread again close to the surface.

Another option is to leave the initial thread tails alone, stitch completely around the shape, and slightly overlap stitches at the end. **Then pull all thread tails to the back side of the work and tie them off with a square knot.**

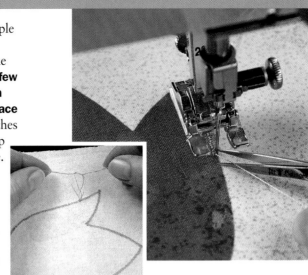

Satin Stitch Appliqué

Satin stitch is done on raw-edge appliqué shapes (see page 20). **This stitch can blend into the appliqué or stand out as a decorative accent, depending upon the look you prefer.** Set the stitch width at 2 and the length between ½ and 1 for a narrow and slightly open stitch. This allows better flexibility when stitching around curves and helps to prevent a knotty look that can occur with a more tightly packed stitch. **The stitches should fall so that the needle is going into the background with the right swing and into the appliqué with the left swing.**

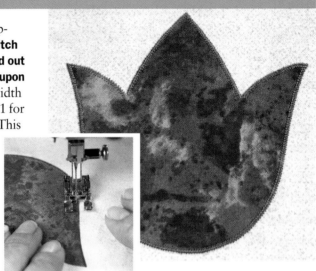

Needle & Thread for Satin Stitch

Try any of the following thread and needle combinations to vary the look of your satin stitching.

- 50 wt. silk finish cotton thread with a 70/10 or 80/12 needle.
- 60 wt. cotton embroidery thread with an 60/8 or 70/10 needle.
- 40 wt. rayon thread with an embroidery needle.

Adjust the stitch length and width with the various weight threads to create different results.

Straight Stitch Appliqué

Straight stitch appliqué requires prepared-edge shapes (see page 17). Set the stitch length at 2 (12 stitches per inch). **Position the needle so the stitches fall just (about 1/16 inch) inside the folded edges.** With this stitch, you can make a machine knot to start and stop by reducing the stitch length to 0 and stitching in place three times. Then return to your regular stitch length. You can use any of the same needle and thread combinations as described in "Needle & Thread for Satin Stitch," above. Or, for an invisible look, use .004 nylon thread with a universal or embroidery needle.

Tip

Use a single hole or straight stitch throat plate if you have one. It prevents your appliqué from being forced down into the opening.

Blanket Stitch Appliqué

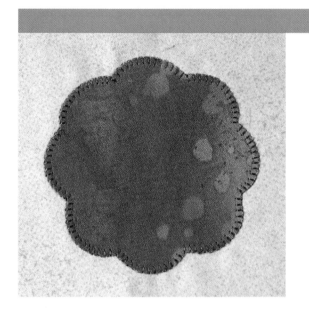

This technique uses raw-edge appliqués. You must have a blanket stitch (sometimes called buttonhole stitch) option on your machine. **The stitch looks like half of a ladder—a line of straight stitches with periodic stitches to the left.** The straight stitches should fall directly along the raw edge of the appliqué, without being on top of it. The side stitches should swing to the left, into the appliqué, and back out again. Get familiar with how many straight stitches your machine takes between each left swing stitch. It will help you manipulate the stitching around curves and points more easily.

Tip

Some machines have a mirror image option to change the swing of a stitch from left to right or vice versa to suit your needs.

Needle & Thread for Blanket Stitch

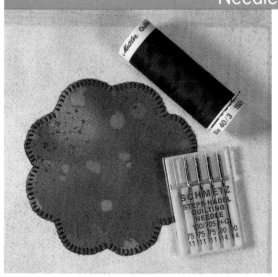

Try using the same needle and thread combinations recommended in "Needle & Thread for Satin Stitch." **Or, for a more primitive look, use a 60 wt. cotton quilting thread with a 90/16 needle.** This heavier thread, especially when used in black, gives the look of folk art hand appliqué. Depending on the thread you use, you may have to vary the machine settings for stitch width and length. Try an initial setting of 2 for both stitch length and stitch width, and adjust up or down from there. Heavier threads can use longer and wider stitches than more delicate threads.

Tip

To create the look of fine *broderie perse* appliqué, use the blanket stitch with 60 wt. cotton embroidery or 100% silk thread.

THE STITCH SAMPLER

Mock Hand Appliqué Method 1

For this technique, use shapes with prepared edges, along with invisible nylon thread and a 70/10 universal or 75/11 embroidery needle. You must also have a blind hem stitch option on your machine. Select the blind hem stitch, then adjust the settings so both stitch length and width are less than 1.

Position the appliqué to the left of the needle so the straight stitches fall along the edge of the appliqué, in the background fabric only. The stitch "bite" that swings to the left should catch only a few threads of the appliqué. Make a practice appliqué and adjust settings as necessary.

Mock Hand Appliqué Method 2

If your machine doesn't have a blind hem option, you can use the zigzag stitch. Use the same thread and needle as for Method 1. Adjust the zigzag settings so both stitch length and width are at 1. **Position the needle so on the right swing it enters the background fabric only, directly against the edge of the appliqué shape. The needle should catch just a few threads of the appliqué on the left swing.** Adjust the stitch width if necessary.

Decorative Stitches

Tip

Refer to your machine's owner's manual for specific instructions for using a double needle. It can't be used with every decorative stitch.

Your machine may have other decorative stitches that could be just wonderful for machine appliqué. **The feather stitch with a fancy rayon or metallic thread is a great accent for appliqués.** Or use a daisy stitch to give a whimsical look to a project. **You can even use a twin needle to jazz up the simple straight stitch technique.** A twin needle can also be effective with several of the decorative stitches.

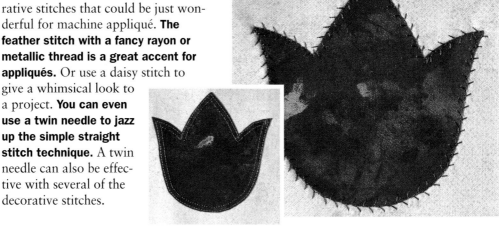

The Quilter's
Problem Solver

Thread Woes

Problem	Solution
Thread breaks when doing specialty stitches.	Sometimes the combination of specialty threads, such as rayon or metallic, with specialty stitches can present a minor problem. It's best to sew slowly when doing this type of stitching. Also, double-check the threading of your machine. If the thread still breaks, try another type of needle. Switch to an embroidery needle if you're using a universal, or try a Metallica needle if the embroidery needle isn't working.
Thread looks bulky where you started and stopped.	Another way to end stitching is to stitch completely around the appliqué with the specialty stitch, such as the blanket stitch. When you reach your starting point, raise the needle out of the fabric, and switch the stitch back to the straight stitch. Shorten the stitch length to about ½, and take three or four of these short stitches to end your work. Remember, you may have to adjust the position of your appliqué under the needle when you switch from one stitch pattern to another.

Skill Builder

Perfect your machine stitches before starting your project.

❏ Stitch a sample of different machine stitches so you can see how each one looks before you commit to a particular stitch.

❏ Try your selected stitch on a sample appliqué to test tension settings, stitch length and width, and your thread choice. Remember to use a stabilizer for your stitching test.

❏ Write on your samples the adjustments you've made for particular stitches, such as shorter or longer stitch length, looser or tighter tension, and even the needle and thread combination used. It will be a handy reference for future machine appliqué projects.

Try This!

Keep bobbins wound and ready to go for machine appliqué. Since you don't need to match bobbin thread to top thread, you can have a few basic colors on hand—white or off-white for light background fabrics, and black or gray for dark backgrounds. To keep these bobbins straight from other bobbins, put a distinctive mark on them with a permanent marker, or keep them in a separate, clearly marked storage box. Bobbinfil and 60 wt. embroidery thread are great for machine appliqué, but you wouldn't want to use them for machine piecing.

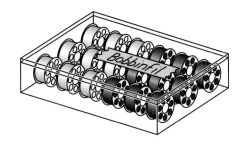

Stitching Perfect
Corners, Curves & Points

H airpin curves . . . sharp left turns . . . serpentines. Sound scary? Don't worry. Instead of being intimidated by angles and curves, plan to meet them head on! After all, even some of the simplest appliqué shapes—stars, hearts, leaves, and flower petals—contain points or curves, and many contain both. No matter how "dangerous" the curves or points may appear, you can master them simply by following the machine appliqué "pointers" on the next pages. You'll be on the road to success in no time!

Getting Ready

Take a good look at your project and analyze the shapes. Do you have a lot of simple shapes with straight edges or gentle curves? Or are there fairly complex shapes with sharp points or hairpin turns? A star is a very good shape to practice stitching points on because it contains both outer points (at the tip of the star points) and inner points (the angles where one star point meets another). And hearts are great for both points and curves. You may find it helpful to practice the following techniques by tracing cookie cutters or shapes from a coloring book onto scrap fabric. Prepare appliqués as needed (freezer paper, fusible web, facings, and so on) for the particular stitch that you'd like to use. Then practice stitching until you feel comfortable with both inside and outside points.

See "Preparing Shapes for Machine Appliqué" on page 16 and "The Stitch Sampler" on page 32 for directions on how to prepare shapes for your preferred appliqué stitch.

See "Preparing Shapes for Machine Appliqué" on page 16 and "The Stitch Sampler" on page 32

What You'll Need

Sewing machine

Open-toe presser foot

Appropriate size and type of needles

Top thread: cotton, rayon, or metallic

Bobbin thread: Bobbinfil or 60 wt. cotton embroidery

Appliqué fabrics

Stabilizer

Fabric scissors

Thread snips or embroidery scissors

Using Satin Stitch

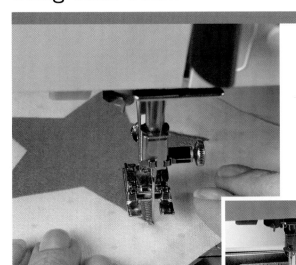

1

Outside corners are stitched using either an overlap or butted technique. For overlap stitching, stitch along the edge of the appliqué until the needle is just off the corner in the *right* swing position. **Lift the presser foot and pivot; lower the foot. Turn the flywheel manually to position the first stitch, which will be to the left. This stitch should be in the appliqué, not the background fabric.** Continue stitching as before.

2

For the butted technique, stitch to the corner until the needle is just off the appliqué in the *left* swing position. Lift the presser foot and pivot. With the foot still up, turn the flywheel manually until the needle switches to the *right* position. **Reinsert the needle into the same hole that it was in before,** and then lower the presser foot. Turn the wheel manually to position the first stitch, which will be to the left. Continue stitching as usual.

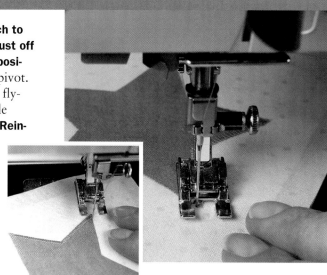

Tip

If your machine has a needle-down feature, use it for optimum control with any of these stopping and pivoting techniques.

3

Inside corners can also be stitched with an overlap or butted technique. **For overlap, stitch along the appliqué until you are the same distance from the corner as the width of your stitch.** For instance, if your stitch is about ⅛ inch wide, stitch until you are ⅛ inch from the inside corner. Stop with the needle in the *left* position. Lift the presser foot and pivot; lower the foot. **Turn the flywheel manually to position the first stitch, which will be to the right. This stitch will be in the appliqué, not in the background.** Continue stitching as before.

4

For inside butted corners, stitch along the edge of the appliqué, and continue stitching past the corner or turning point by the same distance as your stitch width. If your stitch width is ⅛ inch, stitch ⅛ inch past the corner. Stop with the needle in the *right* position, lift the presser foot, and pivot. With the foot up, turn the wheel until the needle switches to the left position. Reinsert the needle into the same hole that it was in before, then lower the presser foot. Turn the flywheel manually to position the first stitch to the right. Continue stitching.

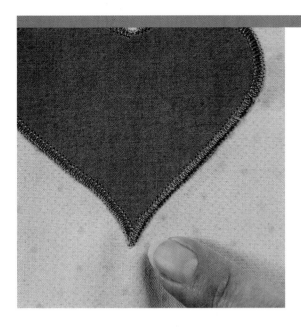

Outside and inside points are similar to corners, but the angles are narrower, making it necessary to make some adjustments to your stitching. **To stitch narrow outside points with the overlapped technique, use a fairly narrow stitch width.** Stitch until the needle is just off of the point in the *left* position. Lift the presser foot and pivot. With the foot up, turn the flywheel manually until the needle switches to the right position. Reinsert the needle into the same hole that it was in before, then lower the presser foot. Turn the wheel manually to position the first stitch, which will be to the left. Continue stitching.

Outside points can also be handled with a tapered stitch. **Sew along the edge of the appliqué until the needle hits the raw edge of the opposite side of the appliqué shape on a left swing of the needle.** Turn the fabric slightly so that the point is centered within the presser foot. Stitch toward the point, continually reducing the stitch width so that it is at 0 by the time you reach the end of the point.

Learning to taper smoothly can be tricky. It pays to practice this on scrap fabric before you reach for your appliqué project.

With the needle down, lift the presser foot and pivot the fabric. **Gradually increase the stitch width as you stitch until it is back to your original width setting.** Continue to stitch as before. The tapered point takes some practice, but the lovely results are worth the time it takes to master it.

Rayon threads create beautiful satin stitches, but if you're just starting out, cotton embroidery thread will call less attention to the less-than-smooth tapers.

PERFECT CORNERS, CURVES & POINTS

8

Inside points can be stitched using either the butted technique or the tapered technique. For butted stitches, appliqué along one side of the point until the needle is even with the opposite edge of the inner point in the *right* swing position. With the needle down, lift the presser foot and pivot. **Position the fabric so the raw edge is centered within the toes of the presser foot. Turn the flywheel to position the first stitch, which will be to the left.**

For tapered stitching, follow Steps 6 and 7 on page 41, as described for tapering outer points.

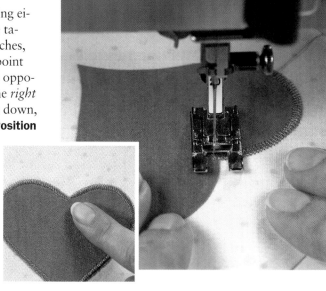

For tapered stitching, follow Steps 6 and 7 on page 41, as described for tapering outer points.

Tip

The tighter the curve, the more frequently you need to stop and pivot for both inner (concave) and outer (convex) curves.

9

To keep a consistent look to your stitches, it's best to use a slightly open zigzag stitch. If your stitches are packed together, they'll look choppy as they go around a curve. **For an *outside* curve, pivot when the needle is in the *right* swing position. For an *inside* curve, pivot when the needle is in the *left* swing position.**

Pivot at consistent intervals, such as every four or five stitches, for a smooth-looking curve.

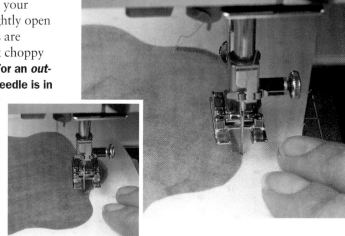

Using Blanket Stitch

1

Both inside and outside points as well as corners require that the blanket stitch "bite" falls perpendicular to the points *exactly* at the point or corner. This will prevent the point from rolling or raveling with wear. Often, to get the stitch to fall exactly at the point of the appliqué, you will need to force the stitch to hit where you want it to. As you approach a point, you may need to create a slight drag on the fabric by holding it so that it doesn't move as far forward as it naturally would with the feed dogs.

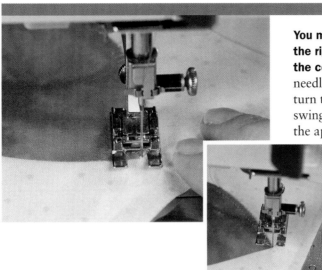

You must stop the needle so it is in the right swing position, exactly at the corner of the appliqué. With the needle down, lift the presser foot and turn the fabric so the needle will swing to the left, taking a bite into the appliqué. **The bite should be exactly in the center, not closer to one edge of the appliqué than the other.** Complete the stitch, letting the needle stitch back to the right position. Pivot the fabric again and continue stitching along the adjacent edge of the appliqué.

Tip

If you have lots of narrow points or small pieces, adjust the stitch length and width from the standard settings. Match the stitch in scale to the appliqué.

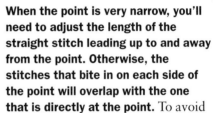

3

When the point is very narrow, you'll need to adjust the length of the straight stitch leading up to and away from the point. Otherwise, the stitches that bite in on each side of the point will overlap with the one that is directly at the point. To avoid that situation, use the flywheel of your machine to raise the needle manually so you can move the fabric a bit further than a regular stitch. The needle should enter exactly at the point, as before. Take the bite stitch, then raise the needle and move the fabric again so the first stitch leading out of the point is longer than normal.

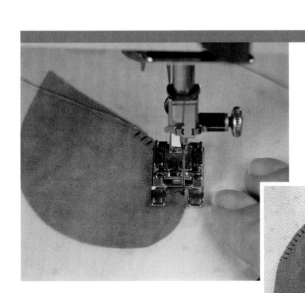

4

As for satin stitching, outside curves are blanket stitched by pivoting the fabric with the needle in the right swing position. Inside curves are stitched by pivoting with the needle in the left swing position. Be sure to pivot when the needle is in the straight stitch mode, not after it has taken a bite into the appliqué fabric. **If you pivot then, the result will be an open V-stitch, rather than two stitches directly overlapping one another.**

PERFECT CORNERS, CURVES & POINTS

Using Mock Hand Appliqué

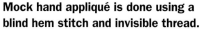

1

Tip

Test-drive your machine, and note how many straight stitches are made between bite stitches for easier planning.

Mock hand appliqué is done using a blind hem stitch and invisible thread. Note: We used colored thread rather than monofilament so you could see the backstitching. (See page 36 for complete details.) Corners and points are handled as in the blanket stitch, since the blind hem stitch also takes a bite into the appliqué fabric. However, the blind hem stitch has more than one straight stitch between the stitches that swing to the left, which makes it a little trickier to stop the straight stitching exactly at the point before the bite stitch is taken.

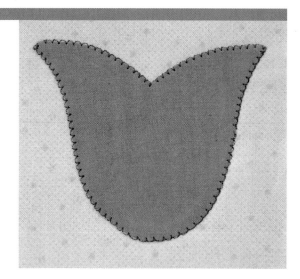

2

Tip

Learn to use the flywheel of your machine as if it were your third arm. It is so helpful in positioning the needle *exactly* where it needs to be.

Because there may be several stitches before the blind hem stitch takes a bite, it is more difficult to control the placement of stitching at corners as you near the corner. **If you are just about at the corner and you still have more than one straight stitch before the bite stitch, you can adjust by reversing the stitching for one or two stitches.** If you have an odd number of stitches to go, you may need to backstitch for one, then use the flywheel to manually adjust the length of the last stitch.

Removing Stabilizer

After you are finished stitching your appliqué in place, you need to remove the stabilizer from the back of the project. **If you are using a simple tear-away–type stabilizer, place your thumb or finger against the stitches to help protect them, and *gently* pull toward the stitches as you remove the stabilizer.** Perforated stabilizers, such as Easy Stitch (shown in our example), make this job really easy and help prevent popped stitches. If you are using another type of stabilizer, refer to the manufacturer's instructions for removal.

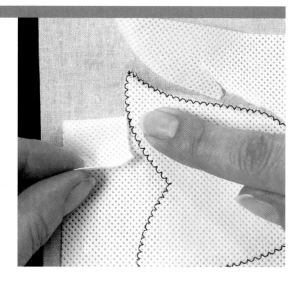

The Quilter's
Problem Solver

Controlling the Stitches

Problem	Solution
Stitches look slanted and uneven around curves.	Many times speed is the culprit. If you sew too fast, you can get ahead of yourself, making it difficult to stop and pivot at the correct spot. If you have a tendency to really step on the gas, set your machine to half-speed or practice using lighter pressure on the foot pedal.
Satin stitching looks bumpy or knotty.	The stitches should lie next to, not on top of, each other. Increase the stitch length slightly to give stitches room to "breathe." Or use a finer thread to reduce the bulk or a satin stitch foot that has a channel underneath for the stitches to pass through. A flat-bottom foot can sometimes cause stitch buildup.
Thread jams at beginning, making an unsightly mess.	Whenever you begin to sew, set the needle by manually lowering it through the fabric *before* you lower the presser foot and press the foot pedal. You may also need to hold the thread tails for the first several stitches to prevent them from knotting.

Skill Builder

For a professional result, remove the background fabric from behind appliqués.

❏ When the background is dark, it will prevent show-through.

❏ Machine stitches are very secure, so it won't cause the background to become unstable.

❏ It makes quilting—by hand or machine—easier to do, especially if you want to quilt on the appliqués themselves.

Turn the project to the back and rub the background between your fingers to separate the layers. Slit only the background fabric with an embroidery scissors, then trim to ¼ inch inside the stitching line.

Try This!

Here's a time-saver that works well on small projects—try quilting as you appliqué! Pin batting and backing behind your project before you begin. Cotton batting will give you the most control. Make sure both the batting and the backing are larger than your appliqué background, as with any quilt sandwich. Appliqué using whatever stitch you prefer. If you notice any skipped stitches, switch to a larger-size needle to accommodate all the layers. By the time the appliquéing is finished, all you have to do is add the background quilting and the binding!

Bias Stems, Vines & Basket Handles

Graceful swoops and flowing curves are part of the immense appeal of appliqué. Bias tubes of fabric are at the heart of those elegant vines and curving basket handles we all admire. An entire quilt style, Celtic appliqué, is based on bias tubes. In case the thought of working bias strips into neat little tubes gives you pause, never fear. Lots of nifty tricks, tips, and tools transform the task of making bias tubing from being drudgery to being amazingly fast and simple.

Getting Ready

Choose fabrics based on how they'll be used in your project. For instance, if you want a realistic-looking vine, select a hand-dyed or mottled fabric rather than a fabric in which the color is consistent throughout. The mottling will add visual depth and mimic nature. Plaid fabrics, on the other hand, make an interesting choice for basket handles, since plaid cut on the bias yields a woven-handle look. Another important factor to consider is the quality of the fabric. Fabrics with high and consistent thread counts work best. The threads in loosely woven fabrics tend to stretch apart, and the fabric looks thin when bias stems are bent.

There are several methods for constructing bias tubes. Read through the entire chapter and decide which method you'll use before cutting bias strips; the method dictates how wide to cut your strips.

What You'll Need

- **Appliqué fabrics**
- **Rotary cutting supplies**
- **Fabric scissors**
- **Thread snips or embroidery scissors**
- **Chalk wheel or pencil**
- **Sewing machine**
- **Open-toe presser foot and zipper foot**
- **Top thread: cotton, rayon, or nylon**
- **Bobbin thread: Bobbinfil or 60 wt. embroidery**
- **Appropriate size and type of needles**
- **Iron and ironing board**
- **Bias press bars**
- **Glue stick, Steam-A-Seam 2, or fusible thread (optional)**
- **Stabilizer**

Cutting Bias Stems

1

Work with a 12-inch square or 12 × 15-inch rectangle of fabric for manageability. Use your rotary-cutting ruler to square up one end of the fabric. **Use the 45 degree line on the ruler to position it diagonally across the fabric.** Cut along the edge of the ruler with your rotary cutter. **From this bias-cut edge, measure the desired width for your bias strips (see Step 1 on page 48), and continue to make parallel cuts.** The bias pieces will become shorter as you near the corners of the fabric, but short strips can be pieced together to make longer bias strips.

 Tip

A 12" square yields approximately 3 yards of ¼" bias tubing, so plan your fabric requirements accordingly.

BIAS STEMS, VINES & BASKET HANDLES

2

Tip

It's more accurate to align the ruler with a marked straight line than with a hand-cut edge, so mark all lines first, then cut.

If you prefer to use scissors instead of a rotary cutter, try this method for cutting strips. Using the same size square or rectangle of fabric, fold over one edge of the fabric to meet the bottom edge, creating a 45 degree angle. Finger press the fold, or press it lightly with an iron. **Open up the fabric and cut along the fold with scissors. Using a ruler, measure the desired width of your strips from the bias-cut edge, and mark the line with a chalk wheel or pencil.** Continue to mark and cut with scissors across the fabric.

3

Tip

If you plan to use bias bars (see below), you may prefer to press the seams to one side. That way the bias bar won't get hung up on them.

If you need longer bias strips than your cut lengths, sew them together to make longer strips. Hold two strips with right sides together so they are perpendicular to one another, and their bottom edges are even. The strips will form a 45 degree angle. **Offset the strips by ⅜ inch, as shown. Stitch across the strips with a ⅜-inch seam, backstitching at each end.** Press the seam open to reduce bulk.

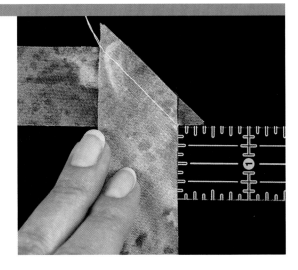

Bias Press Bars

1

Bias press bars are available in a variety of sizes from ⅛ to 1 inch, all in one package. There are two good reasons to use bias press bars—they let you make bias tubes that are accurately sized, and they help save your fingertips from getting uncomfortably close to the hot iron (a hazard when you fold your own bias tubes).

Calculate the width to cut bias strips by doubling the finished size, then adding ½ inch for seam allowances and ⅛ for ease. For instance, if you want ¼-inch finished bias, cut strips 1⅛ inches wide (¼ + ¼ + ½ + ⅛).

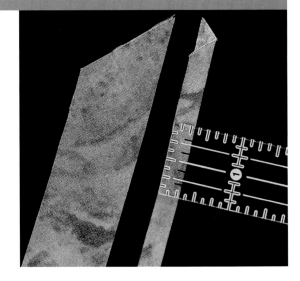

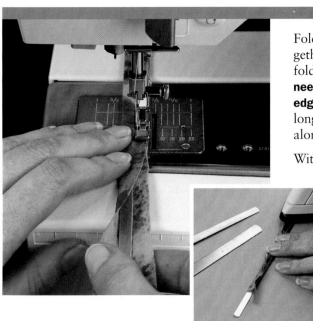

Fold the fabric with *wrong* sides together, and lay the bias bar inside the fold. **Using a zipper foot, stitch so the needle enters the fabric along the edge of the bias bar.** If the fabric is longer than the bias bar, slide the bar along as you go.

With the press bar still in the tube, roll the seam so it is centered underneath the bar. Trim the seam if it extends beyond the edges of the bar. **Press both seam allowances to one side, not open, moving the bar along inside as you go.** Remove the bar, and press the tube again for flat, crisp edges.

Tip

Bias press bars are available in metal and heat-resistant nylon. Metal can give a flatter result, but nylon is cooler on your fingers!

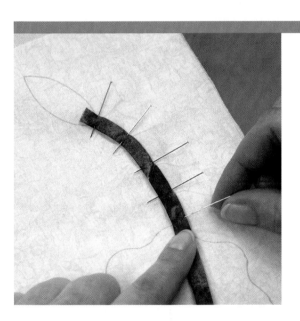

Center the stem over the drawn placement line on the background fabric. **You may choose to pin it in place, or you can hand or machine baste it in place with a running stitch down the center of the stem.** A glue stick also comes in handy for holding stems and vines in place. **To hide raw ends, allow a little extra at each end to tuck under other appliqués.** Then, using your favorite machine appliqué technique, stitch in place.

Tip

Don't forget to use stabilizer underneath the background fabric when machine sewing stems or vines in place.

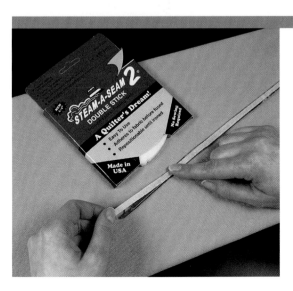

Another way to "baste" bias tubes in place is with Steam-A-Seam 2. It's a fusible product that comes packaged, by the yard, or as a narrow strip on a roll—which is the type you want for bias tubes. **Steam-A-Seam 2 is tacky on one side, so you can stick it to the fabric with simple pressure. Center the strip on the wrong side of the bias stem;** it doesn't need to cover the full width. Once the fusible strip is in place, position the bias tube on the background fabric. Fuse it in place with a damp press cloth or light steam. Stitch as desired.

Tip

If the Steam-A-Seam 2 is wider than your bias tubes, cut it in half lengthwise to make two usable pieces.

BIAS STEMS, VINES, & BASKET HANDLES

Making Bias without Bars

1

Tip

Use a hot, dry iron, being careful not to stretch the fabric as you press.

You can also make bias strips without bias press bars. If you don't have press bars, cut bias strips three times the finished width of the finished stem, vine, or basket handle. Lay the strip right side down on the ironing board. Fold one-third of one long edge of the strip to the wrong side and press. **Fold the other long edge in a similar manner, so the raw edge is hidden just inside the first fold, and press again.**

2

Tip

Premade, 100% cotton bias is available by the yard in a variety of colors at many quilt shops. You can attach it just like hand-made bias.

Here's another way to fold bias strips that works well when you need bias tubes that are ¼ inch or wider. Cut strips three times the desired finished width. With wrong sides together, press the strip in half. **Then fold raw edges over so they are centered underneath the bias strip, between both folds. Press.**

3

Tip

If the bias tends to roll away from the needle as you blindstitch, control it by using a slightly wider blindstitch.

To attach bias that you folded by hand, open the last fold and lay the crease along the drawn placement line on the background fabric. **Using a straight stitch and thread that matches the bias fabric, sew in the fold.** When finished, refold the bias so it covers the stitching and all raw edges. **Using blind hem stitch appliqué (see page 36), stitch the remaining side of the stem to the background.** If you are using a satin, blanket, or straight stitch for your project, stitch on both sides of the bias so both sides of the stem or vine look complete.

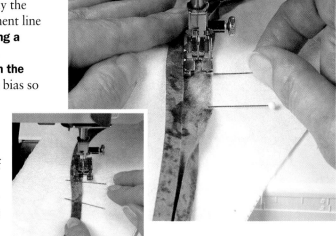

The Quilter's
Problem Solver

Bumps and Ripples around Curves

Problem	Solution
Stems buckle at the curves when stitching them.	If possible, stitch any *inside* curves first. This allows the bias to relax along the outer edge and lie more smoothly. If you have a vine that meanders in both directions, you can baste in place, then stitch just the inside curves on both sides of the vine. Go back and finish by stitching the outer curves on each side.
Completed stems or handles look bumpy, not smooth.	Because they are made of fabric cut on the bias, the weave within the stems can easily shift. Place a clean, damp press cloth over the stems or handles, and press well. This helps tighten things up and make the fabric lie flat. This pressing method is actually great for all appliquéd areas. But use caution—nylon thread can take *some* heat when using a press cloth, but always test it first!

Skill Builder

Many times you can add even more interest to a project through embellishing. Use rayon thread and simple stitching to create veins in leaves and add texture or shading to stems. Experiment with machine embroidery techniques to stitch curly tendrils along the edges of a vine.

Does your machine have the ability to stitch embroidery motifs? If so, look for images like bees, butterflies, or birds, and use them to create a realistic or whimsical touch.

Try This!

If your project calls for lots of stems or vines, you may want to try this slick trick—use fusible thread to baste your stems in place. Thread it through the machine as usual and use cotton thread in the bobbin. Stitch directly on top of the drawn placement line on the background fabric. This places a fine line of "glue," which will become activated by heat. Now center the bias stem in place on top of the fusible thread, and press into place following the package directions. Add satin, blanket, or blind hem stitching, as desired.

BIAS STEMS, VINES & BASKET HANDLES

51

olorful stained glass appliqué takes its name from a time-honored art form—leaded stained glass. While the results of this method may look intricate or complex, stained glass appliqué is actually quite easy. It's fuss-free—and there's no risk of cutting your hands on a shard of glass! Instead, you simply arrange bits of fabrics to form a mosaic pattern, which can be either realistic or abstract. The fabric patches are separated and secured by strips of black bias "leading."

Getting Ready

To get started with stained glass appliqué, you'll need two things—a pattern and folded black bias. (Of course, you can buck the traditional and use whatever color bias you like!)

Stained glass appliqué patterns are available at quilt shops and through mail order. You can also draw your own designs. If you're just getting started with this technique, a good place to look for inspiration is in pattern books for actual stained glass. You may find a design you'd like to use or an idea that you can adapt for fabric.

You can either make your own black bias, or, to make your project particularly quick and easy, consider using purchased bias tape. Look for 100 percent cotton tape, and be sure to buy single fold, not double fold, tape. Ready-made iron-on bias tape is easiest of all.

For directions on making folded bias strips, see "Bias Stems, Vines & Basket Handles" on page 46. There's no need to sew a bias tube. That will only add bulk.

For directions on making folded bias strips, see "Bias Stems, Vines & Basket Handles" on page 46.

What You'll Need

- **Stained glass appliqué pattern**
- **Stabilizer *or* lightweight nonfusible interfacing**
- **Permanent marker**
- **Freezer paper**
- **Craft or paper scissors**
- **Iron and ironing board**
- **Appliqué fabrics**
- **Silk pins**
- **Fabric scissors**
- **Water-soluble glue stick**
- **Black fabric to make bias strips, or premade bias tape**
- **Bias bars (optional)**
- **Sewing machine**
- **Open-toe embroidery foot**
- **Black cotton thread or smoke-colored mono-filament**
- **Rotary-cutting supplies**

Stained Glass Appliqué

1

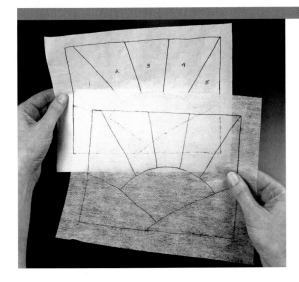

Trace the pattern onto stabilizer or nonfusible interfacing. This will be the sewing foundation for the appliqué. **Then trace the same pattern onto freezer paper.** The freezer paper pattern will be cut apart and used as templates for cutting the individual fabric patches. Transfer labels onto the freezer paper pattern so you can easily assemble the patches in the appropriate order. If your pattern isn't labeled, simply number the segments so you'll know which piece goes where in the final arrangement.

2

Press the freezer paper templates onto the *right* side of your fabrics. If you press them to the back of the fabric, your final piece will be the reverse of your original pattern. Cut out the shapes along the edge of the freezer paper templates. You don't need to worry about leaving space for seam allowances because the fabric pieces will be butted, not sewn together.

Tip

Keep grain line in mind when you place your templates on the fabric. A wallhanging will hang nicer if the outer edges aren't cut on the bias.

3

Arrange the fabric patches on top of the stabilizer foundation. Don't worry if pieces don't precisely match the drawn lines. Any minor gaps will be covered by the bias "leading" that you will be adding. Pin or hand baste the patches in place. Or use a dab of glue stick on the back of each patch to secure it.

Tip

Place pins in the center of the patches, away from where you will be sewing. That way you won't have to remove them as you stitch.

4

Cut a section of bias that is long enough to cover the first joint where two patches meet. If you're using premade bias, make sure you don't use a section that contains a seam. **Center the bias over the joint. Pin or hand baste the bias in place.** Be sure to start placing bias on the shorter seams that will be overlapped by longer, intersecting pieces. The goal is to have all ends of bias overlapped by other pieces. Of course, the bias tape ends at the edges of the block or quilt top will not be overlapped until a border or binding is attached.

Tip

A really quick way to "baste" the bias in place is to use fusible bias tape, which is sold expressly for this purpose.

5

Using your open-toe embroidery foot, stitch the bias in place with a straight stitch. Stitch close to the edge of the bias to secure it and the fabric underneath it to the foundation. Use black cotton thread or smoke-colored monofilament. If you prefer, you can hand appliqué the bias tape in place.

If you are using iron-on bias tape, you must still stitch it in place, just as with regular bias tape or strips.

6

For curved sections, baste the bias in place with thread or pins. Then stitch the inner curve in place first. If you stitch the outer curve first, the inside curve may buckle, and you'll end up stitching pleats into the bias.

Once the inner curve is stitched, sew the outer curve in place.

To prevent puckering, stitch the outer curve in the same direction as the inner curve.

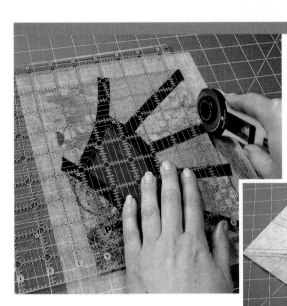

7

After you have attached all bias and all appliqué pieces are secured, **square up the edges of the quilt top with a rotary cutter and ruler.**

After trimming, you can tear away the foundation material to reduce the bulk and stiffness in the finished project.

Attach borders if desired, or quilt. If your project has no borders, it's nice to bind the quilted piece with black binding to complete the look of leaded stained glass.

QUICK & EASY STAINED GLASS APPLIQUÉ

Molas are a form of reverse appliqué (where the fabric on top is cut out to reveal another fabric underneath) developed by the Cuna people of the San Blas Islands, near Panama. Their intricate folk art stitchery is widely used on both the fronts and backs of festive-colored clothing. Quilt teacher and author Jane Hill has adapted the Cuna technique so you can quickly and easily produce this type of ethnic-inspired appliqué with fusible web and a sewing machine. Create your own brightly colored Mola to decorate a shirt, make a pillow top, design a quilt block, or frame as artwork.

Getting Ready

A Mola is made by cutting channels out of a fabric so that other fabrics underneath show through. Solid fabrics work best for this type of work because the channels are so narrow. Prints tend to blur the lines between the layers. To duplicate the look of an authentic Cuna Mola, look for bright, pure colors.

Because a Mola is made by doing intricate cutwork, a very sharp pair of embroidery scissors is a must. Cut the design and foundation fabrics slightly oversize from your finished dimensions. You can trim away frayed edges after all cutting, fusing, and decorative stitching is completed.

In addition to the Mola pattern on page 60, a great source for Cuna-inspired Mola patterns is *The Electric Mola* by Jane Hill, available in quilt shops or by ordering directly from Hillcraft Needle Arts in Boca Raton, Florida (phone: 561–395–3321).

What You'll Need

- **Mola pattern**
- **Paper-backed fusible web**
- **Pencil**
- **Assorted bright-color fabrics for design, foundation, and inlays**
- **Iron and ironing board**
- **Thread snips or embroidery scissors**
- **White chalk marking pencil**
- **Press cloth**
- **Sewing machine with zigzag or decorative stitches**
- **Rayon embroidery thread to match design layer**
- **Cotton thread for bobbin (match top thread)**
- **Variety of rayon embroidery thread for machine embroidery**
- **Embroidery floss for hand embroidery (optional)**

Creating a Mola

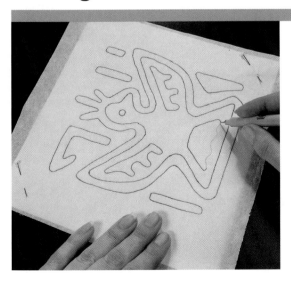

1

Cut a piece of paper-backed fusible web that is 2 inches smaller than the design layer so it won't accidentally get fused to the ironing board. Center it over your design with the paper side facing up. **Using a pencil, trace the design onto the paper side of the fusible web.** The finished design will be a mirror image of the tracing. If you want the design to face in the reverse direction, first trace it on a plain sheet of paper. Then use a light box or sunny window to trace the design from the wrong side of the paper onto the fusible web.

Tip

The smooth side is the paper side; the rough side is the adhesive or fusible side of paper-backed web.

Center the fusible design in the middle of the *wrong* side of the design layer fabric. Follow the manufacturer's directions to fuse the traced design onto the design layer fabric (royal blue fabric, in our example).

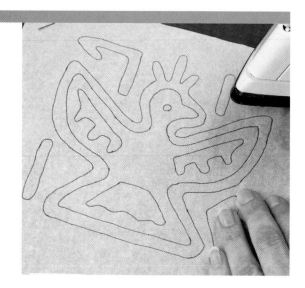

Tip

Fold the design on a straight line to begin cutting. If you snip into a curved line, you'll get a V-shaped snip instead of a straight one.

To cut the Mola design into the design layer fabric, **fold the tracing on a straight line in the design. Cut a small snip on the fold with your embroidery scissors.**

Then insert the tip of your scissors into the slit you just made, and carefully cut completely around the traced design, until the piece is completely cut away from the design. Be sure to cut only on the lines. Do not cut from one line to another, or you'll be cutting through your design layer. Repeat this procedure until you have cut on every drawn line.

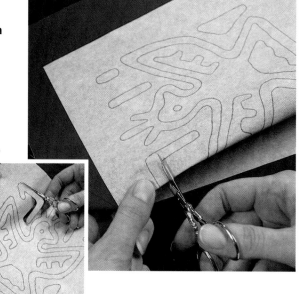

The large piece you are left with is your design layer. After cutting the design, this layer will resemble a piece of Swiss cheese! The extra pieces that fall away when cutting may be saved and used as positive appliqués (fabric that gets appliquéd or fused on top of another, as opposed to the reverse or cutwork appliqué technique). See "Try This!" on page 61 for an example.

Remove the fusible web from the back of the design layer. **Turn the design layer right side up and place it on top of the foundation layer** (gold fabric, in our example). *Do not press.*

At this point, all the channels you cut out of the royal blue fabric have the same color foundation fabric showing through. To create a more colorful design, you can place inlay fabrics or accent pieces between the layers, as described in Step 6.

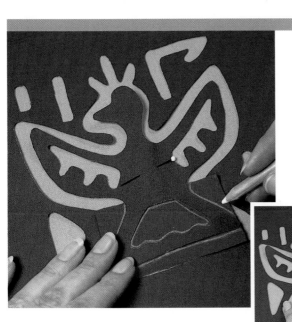

Prepare inlay fabric by applying fusible web to the wrong side of each piece. Slide one of the pieces between the design and foundation layers so it shows through the "windows" in the design layer. **Use a white chalk marking pencil to outline the inlay shape.** Slip out the inlay fabric and cut out the inlay shape, cutting slightly outside the marked lines. **Replace the inlay, making sure it doesn't extend into any windows where you don't want it.**

Use the tip of a straight pin to adjust the placement of inlays easily.

 Tip

Once you have finalized your design with all inlays where you want them, cover the design with a press cloth. Press following the manufacturer's directions for your fusible web. The web will bond all three layers together, and you're ready for the final decorative stitching.

Tip

Build your Mola on a square rotary ruler or flat cookie sheet. It's easy to carry to the ironing board where you can slide it off for fusing.

THE ELECTRIC MOLA

Tip

See "The Stitch Sampler" on page 32 for details on each type of stitch.

Use rayon embroidery thread in the machine needle and cotton thread in the bobbin. Select the blanket stitch, blind hem stitch, or zigzag stitch. Reduce stitch length to 2 (12 stitches per inch) and the stitch width to 2 (or slightly narrower than the normal setting). Stitch around every cut edge in the design. **If you use a blanket or blind hem stitch, make sure the stitch length falls on the foundation layer and the stitch width catches the design layer. The bite of the stitch width should be at least three threads deep into the design fabric.** Adjust your stitch width if necessary.

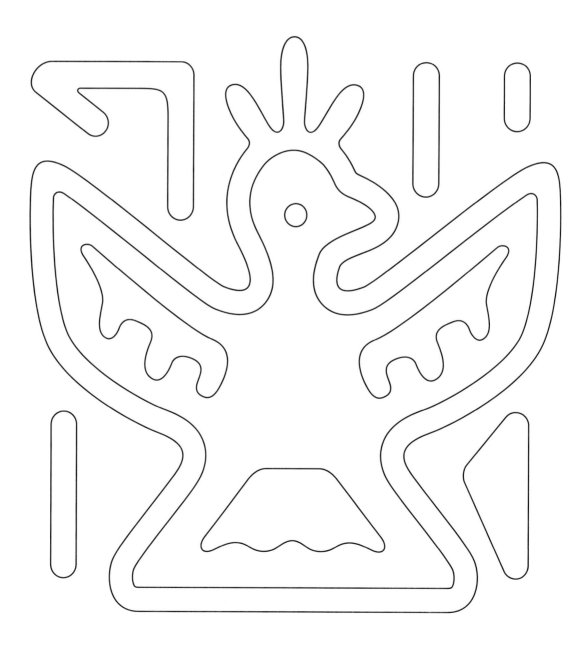

The Quilter's
Problem Solver

Working with Fusible Web

Problem	Solution
Paper backing is hard to remove.	Sometimes it's hard to get a grip on the paper backing to peel it off the fabric. Scratch a small X on the paper with a straight pin. Bend the paper along the cut, and peel the backing away.
Needle sticks when stitching through fusible web.	Make sure you are using a lightweight product that is sewable. Heavy-duty fusible webs cannot be stitched through by machine. Also, since you'll be using a fine rayon thread, switch to an machine embroidery needle. This type of needle is made for using decorative threads such as rayon, and the extra-sharp point will pierce through the web more easily.

Skill Builder

Go beyond the basics with these creative and colorful ideas.

❑ Add decorative machine stitches to enhance the design. If you're not familiar with all of your machine's decorative stitches, make a stitch sampler to audition them. Choose stitches you like for stitching in the window areas or on top of the design layer.

❑ Hand embroider designs using three to six strands of embroidery floss and simple running stitches, cross-stitches, or other embroidery stitches.

❑ Add more than one accent color for inlays.

❑ Create your own Mola designs. Start with a simple drawing, such as the outline of a cat. Make a double outline so you can cut a channel, then add other elements to the design.

Try This!

Customize your Mola with these ideas.

❑ Instead of using inlays to add new colors to your design, try using a colorful print or a bold stripe as the foundation layer (still use a solid fabric on top).

❑ Enlarge or reduce the design at a copy center to suit your needs.

❑ Save the pieces left over after cutting out the windows. They have fusible web on them, so you can use them to make a positive appliqué design that complements the Mola.

Tools, tools, tools! The quilter's world is full of charming, elegant, and useful tools that can make appliqué easy and enjoyable. Let well-known quilt teacher Susan McKelvey guide you through the necessities for hand appliqué, all of which are affordable and easy to find at your local quilt shop or in your favorite quilt-supply catalog. There's nothing more delightful than sitting down to appliqué in a comfortable chair in a quiet, sunlit spot, knowing you have everything you need at your fingertips.

Getting Ready

Keep your notions in a special hand appliqué sewing box small enough to transport conveniently. Keep the box where you can pick it up when you can fit in some time to appliqué.

On any particular project, plan ahead. Prepare your fabric, mark it, and organize it. Sandwich bags are wonderful for storing the pieces for appliqué, while large freezer bags hold entire blocks, keeping them clean as well as ensuring against the loss of tiny fabric leaves and berries. Mark the bags with a permanent marker for easy reference, and keep them in your sewing box with the tools where they can wait for your free moments.

When you do appliqué, make sure to work in a well-lit area. If your only chance to appliqué is in the evening, you can duplicate the effect of natural sunlight with an Ott Light. This full-spectrum light is lightweight and portable, and it comes in tabletop, floor, and clamp-on models.

What You'll Need

- **Appliqué fabrics**
- **Thread to match appliqués**
- **Needles: sharps, straws, or milliner's**
- **Needle threader (optional)**
- **Silk or appliqué pins**
- **Embroidery scissors**
- **Paper or craft scissors**
- **Freezer paper or template plastic**
- **Fabric and template markers**
- **Thimble**
- **Thread holder**
- **Support pillow**
- **Pincushion**
- **Emery**

Selecting Supplies for Hand Appliqué

Fabrics and Threads

For traditional appliqué, 100 percent cotton fabric is ideal because it can be easily finger-creased. Prewash and iron before using it. Silk looks wonderful, but it's more difficult to control. Wool and felt can be used for primitive appliqué. See page 98 for more on these specialty fabrics.

Cotton machine embroidery thread is preferred by many experts. Silk or silk-covered cotton makes a fine stitch, and cotton-covered polyester, which is readily available in many colors, works well, too. **Match the thread color and fabric as closely as possible.** If you can't match exactly, use thread a shade darker than your fabric, or use gray thread, which tends to disappear.

Tip

If you plan to do a lot of floral appliqué, buy all shades of green thread for leaves, stems, and vines.

Needles

Tip

With hand sewing needles, the bigger the number, the smaller the needle.

A long, slender needle works best for hand appliqué. **Most quilters experienced in hand appliqué prefer sharps, straws, or milliner's needles.** Beginners may want to start with a #10, which has a large eye for easy threading and doesn't bend. As you gain proficiency, try a #11. It bends more easily, but it is so slender that it slips through fabric as if it were butter. **A needle threader helps thread the tiny eyes of these needles.**

Pins

Tip

Instead of straight pins, you can use ¾" brass-plated safety pins to "baste" appliqué elements in place.

People who hand appliqué agree that they want sharp and slender pins. Beyond that, personal preferences vary. Some prefer silk pins or long, superfine pins such as Iris, while some like short pins, such as sequin pins or pleater pins. Glass head pins are easy to grasp and pull out, while tiny headed pins snag your thread less easily. Try a variety of different pins as you practice your stitching to find out which type is right for you.

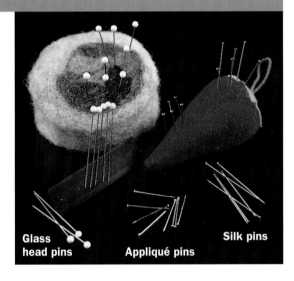

Glass head pins   Appliqué pins   Silk pins

Scissors

Tip

To keep your paper and fabric scissors separate forever, mark them with different ribbons on the handles—white for paper and a color for fabric.

To make it easy to cut small pieces of fabric and clip tiny points, use small, sharp scissors such as 4-inch or 5-inch knife edge or embroidery scissors. These scissors have very pointy, sharp tips, so keep them in a leather sheath or old eyeglass case to prevent them from poking into your work inside your sewing basket.

Ideally, have two pairs of scissors handy—one for fabric and one for template plastic and paper. The scissors you use for template making should be pointed, too, as you'll need to cut templates as accurately as the fabric.

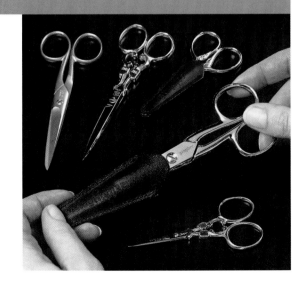

Template-Making Supplies

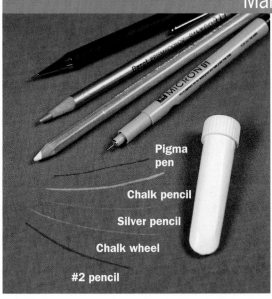

Freezer paper can be ironed onto fabric repeatedly, which makes it a wonderful template material. Template plastic also has several advantages. First, it is translucent, so you can control its placement on fabric. Second, it is hard, making it easy for you to mark around its edges.

To mark templates, choose a permanent marker designed for smooth, shiny surfaces. **The Identipen with its two different-sized points is excellent for marking both freezer paper and template plastic.**

Markers for Fabric & Templates

There are a wide variety of marking tools that you can use to mark appliqué pieces. Chalk markers come in several colors, allowing you to choose the best color for a particular fabric. If your project will take a long time or require a lot of handling, chalk markers may rub off, so consider other options. A #2 pencil works well on light fabrics and is permanent; a mechanical pencil makes a more delicate line. On dark fabrics, try Berol Prismacolors or a quilter's silver pencil. The Pigma pen, size .01, makes a delicate, permanent line on medium colors. It's particularly good for marking prints.

Pigma pen

Chalk pencil

Silver pencil

Chalk wheel

#2 pencil

Additional Tools

Other handy tools for hand appliqué include a thimble, a thread holder to tend several spools, a support pillow (one with a cushion on one side and a flat, smooth surface on the other allows you to pin and adjust your fabric), and a large pincushion and emery to keep needles and pins sharp. You may prefer a tiny pincushion to wear on your wrist, finger, or pinned to your blouse so that you can move pins in and out of the fabric quickly without reaching. Appliqué is a great take-along project, so if you're on the go, a portable project bag is a must.

Tip

A felted wool pincushion keeps needles and pins sharp.

EVERYTHING FOR HAND APPLIQUÉ

Preparing Shapes
for Hand Appliqué

I t's always fun to get started on a new project. But before you can settle into your favorite spot and start stitching, you need to take time to choose your fabrics and prepare your shapes. While making shapes may not be the glamorous job of appliqué, it's nevertheless very important. Your finished appliqué will only be as beautiful and precise as the pieces you start with! So try out the various ways to make appliqué shapes to see which gives you the satisfying results you're looking for.

Getting Ready

It feels great to be organized! Take a little time to get everything ready, and hand appliqué will be a pleasure. This chapter shows you how to prepare and baste your appliqué shapes using several different methods. You may not need all the supplies listed here once you decide on your preferred method, but you will need them to try the various techniques. Start by making plastic templates, and you can use them for preparing needle-turn pieces, traditional appliqué pieces, or freezer paper patterns.

In addition, have your fabrics ready to go. Prewash or test them for colorfastness before using them in appliqué so you won't have a problem with bleeding in the finished project.

What You'll Need

Template plastic

Appliqué pattern

Fine-tip permanent marker

Paper or craft scissors

Appliqué fabrics

Sharp pencil or fabric marker

Fabric scissors

Embroidery scissors

Appliqué needle of choice

Basting thread

Freezer paper

Stapler

Iron and ironing board

Water-soluble glue stick

Plastic circle template

Heavy paper

Preparing Plastic Templates

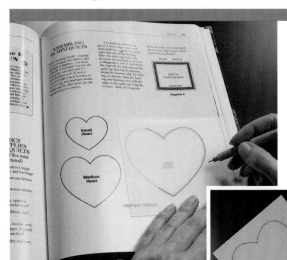

Plastic templates are accurate and durable, especially when you need to make repeated shapes for appliqué. Place a piece of template plastic directly over your appliqué pattern. **Using a fine-tip permanent marker, trace the appliqué piece exactly on the design line.**

Carefully cut out the plastic template on the traced line, using your paper or craft scissors. As you cut, do not add seam allowances on the template plastic. When cutting curved shapes, hold the scissors steady and turn the template plastic, rather than vice versa, for a nice smooth cut.

 Tip

If your template has any little rough edges, smooth them with a nail file.

2

Use the fine-tip permanent marker to write important information on the template. This includes the pattern name, the piece number or name, and how many pieces to cut. This information will keep you organized, and you won't have to refer back to the original pattern to find it.

3

Use the plastic templates to prepare fabric shapes for needle-turn appliqué. **Place the plastic template face up on the right side of the fabric. Trace around the template using a sharp pencil or fabric marker, such as a Pigma pen, size .01.** Cut out the appliqué fabric shape, adding a scant ¼-inch seam allowance around the markings. As you appliqué, the seam allowance will be turned under with your needle to create the finished edge of the appliqué piece. See page 78 for complete directions on needle-turn stitching.

Basted Shapes

1

The same plastic templates are also used to prepare fabric shapes for traditional basted appliqué. Place the plastic template face up on the right side of the fabric, and trace around the template using a sharp pencil or Pigma pen as before. **Cut out the appliqué fabric shape, adding a scant ¼-inch seam allowance around the markings.**

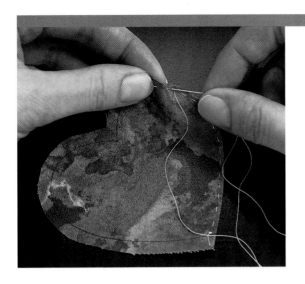

To baste the edges in place, turn the seam allowance under so that the marked line disappears to create the finished edge on the appliqué piece. Use a milliner's or sharp needle and white or light-colored sewing thread to baste. **While you baste, keep the right side of the fabric facing you so you can see that the markings are completely turned under and not visible.**

The closer the stitches are to the folded edge, the easier it is to create smooth shapes. Basting in too far causes puckers and sharp edges.

Freezer Paper on Top

Lots of hand appliquérs like to use freezer paper to prepare appliqué shapes because it gives support to the appliqués as you stitch them to the background fabric. **Place the freezer paper, shiny side down, directly over the appliqué pattern.** Use a sharp pencil to trace the appliqué piece. **Use paper scissors to cut out the freezer paper piece exactly on the traced line.**

If you need several of the same shape, you can cut layers of freezer paper—up to four at once. Trace the design on one piece of freezer paper. Cut three other pieces the same size and stack them with the marked piece on top. Staple the layers together, placing the staples around the edge of the design. **As you cut out the design, your pieces will be accurate and the stapled freezer paper will fall away.** If your design is repeated many times, first make a plastic template, then trace around the plastic template onto the freezer paper for more accurate shapes.

3

Iron the freezer-paper template to the right side of the fabric. Cut out the fabric, adding a ¼-inch seam allowance around the paper. **To stitch the appliqué in place, simply needle-turn the fabric under the paper.** The edge of the paper becomes your turn-under guide. When you have completed stitching the appliqué to the background fabric, gently peel off the freezer paper.

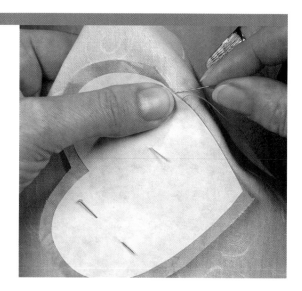

Tip

Let a small fold of fabric show beyond the edge of the paper for perfect placement of your appliqué stitches.

Freezer Paper on Bottom

1

Another way to use freezer paper is as a stabilizer for the shapes. In this method, you baste the appliqué fabric over the freezer paper templates. **Place the shiny side of the freezer paper against the *wrong* side of the appliqué fabric, and press it in place using a hot, dry iron.** If you are ironing several pieces to the fabric, make sure that you leave at least ½-inch spaces between the freezer paper pieces to allow space for seam allowances.

Tip

Flop the pattern before tracing or the finished appliqué will be the reverse of the pattern.

2

Cut out the appliqué fabric. Add a generous ¼-inch seam allowance around the outside edge of the freezer paper as you cut. This seam allowance will be turned over the freezer paper to create the finished edge on your appliqué piece.

Turn the ¼-inch seam allowance over the edge of the freezer paper. Baste it in place by hand with little stitches. Use white or light-colored thread for basting; dark thread may leave little dots of dye on your appliqué piece. Stitch through the paper and two layers of fabric.

Tip

Tiny stitches are hard to remove, but large stitches make it hard to create a smooth edge on the appliqué.

70

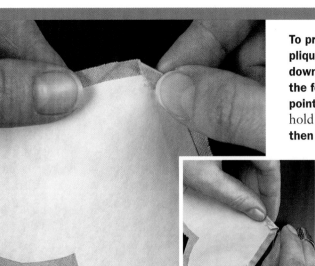

3

To prepare outside points on the appliqué piece, first turn the fabric point down over the freezer paper so that the fold is just beyond the paper point. Use a small dab of glue stick to hold it in place. **Fold the right side, then the left side, tightly over the paper to create a sharp point.** Baste the fabric in place over the paper.

4

Prepare inside points by first clipping the fabric. Use a sharp pair of embroidery scissors, and *do not* clip all the way to the paper. Stop clipping about four threads away from the paper. **Fold the fabric over the paper so that it is taut, then baste the cut edges securely.**

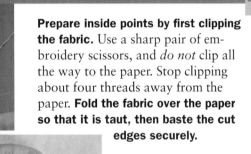

5

When preparing outside, or convex, curves, keep your basting stitches close to the folded edge so that the fabric will curve smoothly. You'll notice that very sharp outside curves have a lot of extra fabric to be folded under, which can create little tucks and points along the edge of the appliqué. **You can prevent these by basting very small running stitches in the fabric seam allowance around the curve. Gently pull the running stitches to bring the seam allowance smoothly over the freezer paper.** Then baste the seam to the freezer paper.

6

Prepare inside, or concave, curves by clipping into the seam allowance so that the fabric will turn neatly over the freezer paper. Clip halfway through the seam allowance, not all the way to the freezer paper.

Make many clips along the edge, evenly spaced (about every ¼ inch or so) and your fabric will form a smooth curve.

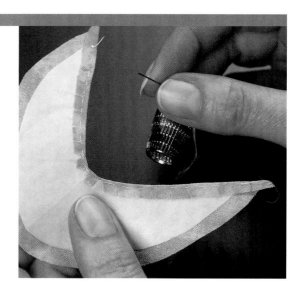

Making Circles

1

Use a plastic circle template available from quilt shops and art-supply stores to draw perfect circles on heavy paper. Use the plastic template to mark and cut out fabric circles that are ½ inch larger than the paper templates to allow for turning under. **Baste around the circle with small running stitches in the seam allowance.**

Tip

Manila folders are the perfect-weight paper for circle templates. For a free source of paper, use the blow-in cards you get in magazines!

2

Place the paper template inside the fabric circle, and pull the basting threads to draw the fabric tight around the paper. Press the fabric circle with steam. When the fabric is cool and dry, remove the paper. Tie a knot in the basting thread, and the circle is ready to appliqué to the background fabric. Don't remove basting until shapes are appliquéd in place.

The Quilter's
Problem Solver

Fraying Edges on Appliqués

Problem	Solution
When preparing shapes, the edges tend to fray.	Some fabrics fray more than others. If one is particularly hard to work with, cut generous ¼-inch seam allowances. You'll have plenty to turn under, and the fabric edges will not fray. Also, don't cut off the extra seam allowance when you prepare outside points. Use your needle to push any extra fabric under the appliqué when you stitch it to the background fabric. A bumpy point is better than a fuzzy point! Use bias fabric grain to your advantage. For instance, cut out heart shapes on the bias. This will place the inside point on the bias and it will fray less than if it were cut on the straight grain.
It's hard to remove the basting thread after shapes are appliquéd in place.	When you start your basting, make sure the knotted end of the thread is on the right side of the appliqué shape, not underneath. You can grip the knot and give it a tug to remove the basting stitch, plus you won't have the lump of a knot stuck under your appliqué.

Skill Builder

Use these tips for creating consistent pieces.

❑ Use a freezer paper technique. You can use the same freezer paper shape several times before its sticking power wears off.

❑ Use a very sharp pencil or a fine-line mechanical pencil to draw on the freezer paper. It takes away the guesswork about which side of a fat line to cut a shape on.

❑ When tracing from a printed pattern, draw exactly on the line. If the line is thick, decide if you'll trace on the inside or outside of the line and do so consistently.

Try This!

You can make perfect circles, every time.

❑ Get ready-made circle templates in the hardware store. Thin plastic or metal washers can be just the right size for appliqué circles. Use them instead of heavy paper for templates.

❑ Use pressure-sensitive dots from the stationery store for circle templates. They're inexpensive and easy to use. You can stick them on fabric and mark around them for needle-turn, or stick them onto template plastic or freezer paper, too.

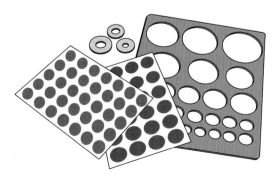

Spray Starch &
Templar Appliqué

K aren Kay Buckley, award-winning quiltmaker and appliqué teacher, shares her secrets for making perfect appliqué shapes using a couple of surprising supplies—heat-resistant templates and spray starch. Anyone who has admired the crisp, clean edges of Karen's appliqué patches knows that the end results are dazzling. This is a surprisingly simple technique equally suited to hand or machine appliqué.

Getting Ready

The whole key to this preparation method is using the firm edge of a heat-resistant template as a pressing guide for your fabric. Templar looks very similar to regular transparent template plastic, but it's a bit thinner. Templar can withstand the heat of an iron, whereas regular template plastic would warp and melt. Be sure to ask specifically for Templar at your quilt shop. It costs a bit more than template plastic, but its ease of preparation for appliqué makes it well worth every penny.

When it comes to buying spray starch, Karen recommends Spray 'N Starch brand because it doesn't leave a stiff-feeling residue on the fabric as some brands do.

What You'll Need

Templar heat-resistant plastic

Appliqué pattern or design

Pencil or permanent marker

Paper or craft scissors

Sandpaper or emery board

Appliqué fabric

Fabric scissors

Iron and ironing board

Spray 'N Starch

Small dish or container

Cotton swabs or small paintbrush

Spray Starch & Templar Appliqué

1

Place Templar over the printed appliqué design, and trace the shape with a pencil or permanent marker. **Using paper or craft scissors, cut the Templar on the lines you just drew.** Do not add a seam allowance to your templates.

Use sandpaper or an emery board to file away any rough spots on the template. This is especially important for super smooth curves.

SPRAY STARCH & TEMPLAR APPLIQUÉ

2

Place the Templar shape on the back of your fabric, and trace around the edge of the Templar with a pencil or an ultra-fine-point permanent marker, such as a Pigma pen, size .01. **Cut out the fabric shape outside the marked lines, adding a ⅜-inch seam allowance to your appliqué shape.**

3

Tip

Work in 3" to 4" sections at a time to prevent the starch from drying.

Place the fabric shape on your ironing board, right side down. Center the Templar template over the wrong side of the fabric shape. Spray a small amount of starch into a small dish. **With a cotton swab or small paintbrush, dab spray starch onto the seam allowance until the fabric is dampened.**

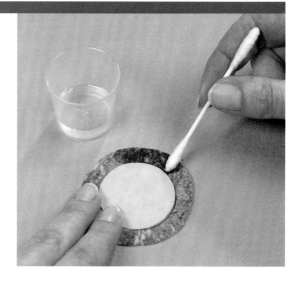

4

Using a hot, dry iron, push the seam allowance up and over the Templar. You will hear a sizzling sound, which means the spray starch is drying. You must keep the iron in place long enough for the starch to dry. When you remove the iron, the seam should lie flat. If the seam pops up, you have not allowed the iron to sit long enough. Press again, but be careful not to press too long or you could scorch the fabric.

5

Every iron is different. You will have to find the best setting on your iron for working with Templar. The iron needs to be hot enough to dry the spray starch but not so hot that it warps the Templar.

If the Templar does warp, it won't harm your iron, but you will need to make a new template.

6

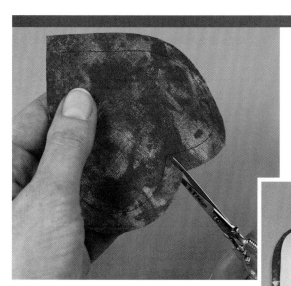

If your shape has inner points, press them first. **To press an inner point, such as in a heart, you'll need to clip the fabric so that the seam allowance can spread in each direction of the two curves.** Clip almost to the marked seam line. After pressing the inner point, work your way around any curved areas.

Tip

It's best to save any outer points, such as leaf points or the tip of a heart, for pressing last.

7

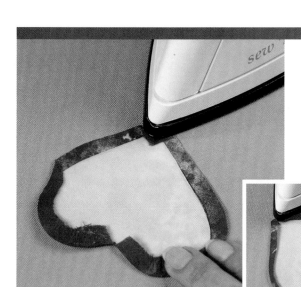

To press an outer point, such as the tip of the heart, first press the seam allowance up over the tip. Then press one side over the Templar completely down to the tip of the point. Repeat, pressing the other side of the point, so the seam allowances overlap. You may need to trim seam allowances if they extend beyond the edge of your finished shape. You can safely trim the seam allowance to as little as 1/16 inch if necessary.

The Perfect
Hand Appliqué Stitch

There's no need to feel as if you're all thumbs when it comes to appliqué. Using something as simple as a wooden toothpick can make an amazing difference in how easily you can create perfect appliqué stitches. With a few other tricks up your sleeve (like how to avoid tangled, knotted thread), you're all set to stitch any appliqué shapes or patterns your heart desires.

Getting Ready

The hand appliqué stitch is the same, regardless of which method you use for turning under the edges on your shapes (needle-turn, freezer paper, Templar, or basted edges). To demonstrate, we'll use needle-turn appliqué, which is appliqué in its most basic form. There's no paper or basting stitches in view to distract from the stitching action.

However, to get ready to try the perfect stitch, prepare your shapes using the method you prefer, get out the matching thread, needles, and your thimble, and you'll be set to go.

Making a Perfect Appliqué Stitch

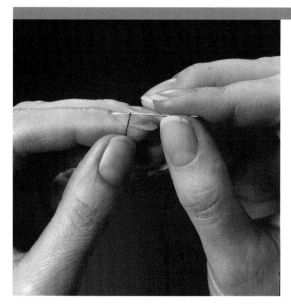

Good hand appliqué starts with preparing a needle and thread for good stitching control. Cut an 18- to 20-inch strand of thread, and thread your appliqué needle. Wind the short end of the thread over your index finger, and hold it firmly in place between your thumb and middle finger. **Gently slide the needle over the surface of your fingernail, and the tip of the needle will pierce the thread.**

Tip

To avoid knots or tangled thread as you take each stitch, try coating your thread with a thin layer of beeswax before threading the needle.

2

Pull gently on the long end of the thread, drawing the pierced portion along the shaft of the needle until the eye of the needle "locks" into position on the thread. This will keep your needle anchored in one place on the thread while you stitch, and it will also help to prevent worn spots or frayed threads and lost needles.

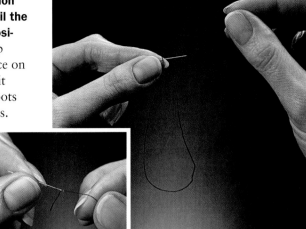

3

Tip

An easy way to follow the motion of the needle and thread is to imagine that you are making a French knot in the air.

To form a knot at the other end of the thread, hold the eye of the needle and the end of the thread together between your right thumb and index finger. Wind the thread two or three times around the needle. **Slide this wound portion of thread gently down the shaft of the needle, so that it lodges between your right thumb and index finger.** Using your left hand, gently draw the needle upward, so that the entire length of thread pulls between your fingers. This will allow the wound portion to create a small knot at the tail end of the thread.

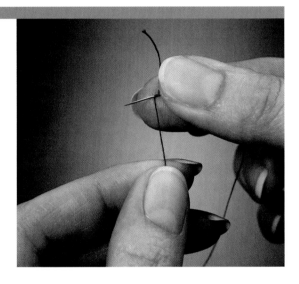

4

To start the first appliqué stitch, place the tip of your needle underneath the appliqué shape only, not the background fabric, approximately at the middle of one side. **Bring the needle up through the fabric, just inside the marked line, and pull the thread all the way through, so that the knot is hidden underneath.**

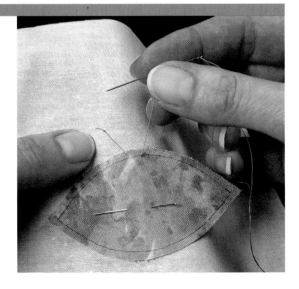

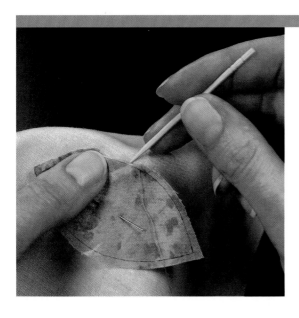

Hold the fabric and appliqué with one hand. With the other, use the tip of the toothpick to gently guide the edge of the fabric under, so that the marked turning line is just out of sight. Crease this fold slightly with your thumbnail, so that you have a neatly turned edge to stitch.

Tip

Don't get too far ahead of yourself. Only turn under a small portion (no more than ¼" to ½") at a time.

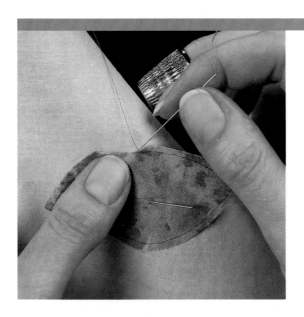

To determine where to insert your needle into the background fabric for the first stitch, pull the thread out at approximately a right angle from the turned edge of the fabric. **Insert the tip of the needle into the background fabric exactly at the point where the thread meets the folded edge.**

Tip

As stitching becomes more natural, you'll know automatically where to insert the needle, without having to pull the thread out at a right angle for every stitch.

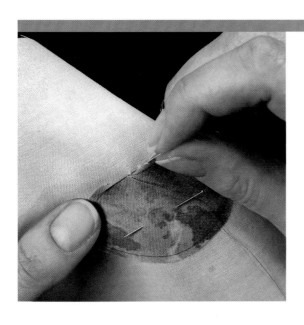

Bring the needle up again through the background fabric, approximately ¹⁄₁₆ to ⅛ inch away, and catch the very edge of the fold in the appliqué. Pull the thread all the way through the fabric, so that your first stitch lodges snugly (but not tightly) into the fabric of the leaf. This creates an almost invisible appliqué stitch. Each stitch you take will be the result of combining Steps 6 and 7 together in one motion. As you practice, experiment to determine the stitch length that gives the results you like best.

THE PERFECT HAND APPLIQUÉ STITCH

Tip

If you stitch with silk thread, you may need to wind the thread four times on the needle to form a large enough knot.

8

To end a thread, insert your needle into the background fabric at the point where you would normally take your next stitch. Bring the thread all the way to the wrong side of your work. **Hold the needle close to the background fabric, and wind the thread around the needle two or three times.**

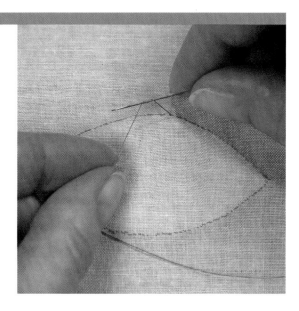

9

With the thread still wound around your needle, insert the tip of the needle between the background and leaf fabrics, as close as possible to the point where your last stitch ended. **Bring the needle all the way out of the fabric about ½ inch away from where you inserted it, allowing a small French knot to form on the surface of the fabric.**

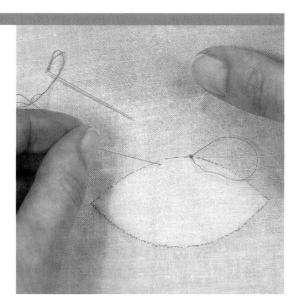

10

Pull on the thread to gently pop the knot out of sight, and clip the end of the thread close to the surface of the fabric. After completing an appliqué design, place the background fabric right side down on top of a terry cloth towel. Spritz the fabric lightly with water, and press it with a hot, dry iron on the cotton setting to give it a crisp, flat finish.

The Quilter's
Problem Solver

Choosing the Right Tools

Problem	Solution
Stitches don't seem to be even.	The most successful hand appliqué stitches are often a result of finding the tools and supplies that suit you best. If a size 11 straw or milliner's needle seems uncomfortable as you stitch, you may be using a needle that is too long for the size of your hand. Try using a shorter one, like a size 11 or 12 sharp, which you may find easier to guide through fabric.
When appliqué fabric is multi-colored, how do you select thread color?	Prints that have lots of colors in them can often make an appliqué design sparkle with life. Stitching from shade to shade within the same fabric is no problem when you use a subtle shade of silk thread. Silk thread is fine and smooth, which makes it "melt" into fabric like butter. Beige, tan, gray, and taupe are good neutrals that will blend beautifully into many different hues.
Thimble feels awkward.	A thimble offers protection from the slim tip of an appliqué needle piercing your fingertip or accidentally slipping under your fingernail (ouch!). If you've tried conventional thimbles and find them clumsy or awkward, you may find help with ThimblePad. It's made of soft, nonslip leather with a reusable adhesive backing. Stick one on your thimble finger for "thimbleless" protection.

Skill Builder

Toothpicks tame the trickiest threads!

Clip the seam allowance up to the marked turning line at the deepest part of an inner point. Appliqué almost up to this point. Run the tip of a toothpick over a water-soluble glue stick, and use the tip to turn under the exposed thread at the point. Give the fabric a slight pinch, so that the glue holds the thread in place. Take a single reinforcement stitch to anchor the thread. Rotate your work, and continue stitching.

Try This!

Avoid tangled, knotted thread with ease.
If you like the way beeswax helps avoid tangles and knots, yet hate the way it clumps on thread or leaves a waxy residue on fabric, try using a product that beaders love. Thread Heaven, a silicone thread conditioner, will coat a strand of thread very lightly and evenly, while making it smooth enough to glide through fabric without snags or snarls. Look for it at your local quilt shop or in mail-order catalogs (see page 15 for sources).

THE PERFECT HAND APPLIQUÉ STITCH

A ll it takes is a needle, a spool of thread, and a little skill to manipulate fabric into all sorts of beautiful shapes. Let teacher Susan McKelvey show you how to make any style curve lie well-rounded and pucker-free. She also shares her methods for making the slimmest of points lie flat—with no bulges allowed. By mastering a few simple techniques, you will be able to fill your quilts with designs of any size and complexity—from delicate details in tiny leaves and flowers to sweeping landscapes of hills and mountains.

Getting Ready

In this chapter, we'll show you how to stitch pointy points and smooth curves using needle-turn appliqué. The same techniques apply to stitching pieces with freezer paper pressed on top. If you prefer freezer paper on the bottom, the edges of your fabric will already be turned under and basted or pressed to the paper to form points or curves, but the stitching techniques will still apply.

Whatever your favorite appliqué method, you need to plan and prepare before you can start stitching. Choose a pattern or design of your own. If you're a beginner and practicing the techniques, try a large heart. It has curves and both inside and outside points, so it makes a wonderful pattern for a first hand-appliqué project. Select, prewash, and iron your fabric. Then draft or trace the templates, mark the fabric for needle-turn, and get your tools ready.

See "Preparing Shapes for Hand Appliqué" on page 66 for details on getting your shapes ready for needle-turn appliqué.

See "Preparing Shapes for Hand Appliqué" on page 66

Stitching Smooth Curves

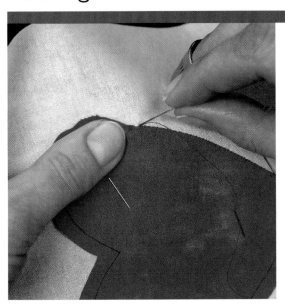

Appliqué shapes are made up of combinations of curves, inside points, and outside points. Before beginning to stitch, examine the piece you are appliquéing and analyze its curves. **Begin sewing on a gradual, fairly long, outside (convex) curve.** This enables you to anchor the piece immediately with fairly straight stitching before you get into the harder curves and points.

Tip

Try pinning shapes from the back, as shown here, so your thread won't catch on the pins each time you take a stitch.

PERFECT POINTS & SMOOTH CURVES

2

Tip

Clip curves with just the tip of sharp embroidery scissors. If you cut further back along the blades, you risk slipping and cutting too far.

Some appliqué pattern directions specify to clip the curves before you stitch them. Remember: Don't clip any more than is absolutely necessary! On outside (convex) curves, you don't need to clip at all. On inside (concave) curves, clip only as needed to ease the seam allowance open. **When clipping, make sure each cut ends a thread or two before the marked seam line.**

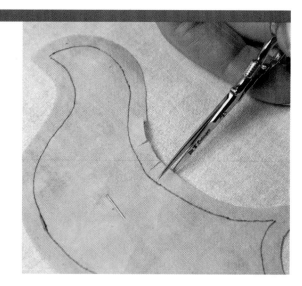

3

Tip

The fatter the seam allowance, the more fabric you'll need to fit under the curve. Trim away excess, leaving as little as 1/16".

Gentle curves are stitched much the same as straight lines—by turning a small portion of the seam allowance and sewing it before moving on. To prepare for sharper curves, however, you need to look 1 to 2 inches ahead of where you're sewing to scout upcoming challenges. **When a sharper curve is nearing, fold under the seam allowance with a toothpick and pin the folds in place.** If you don't pin ahead at the major curves, you can end up with a wad of fabric to turn under all at once, which is impossible to do smoothly.

4

As you get close to a pin, use the point of your needle to ease the fabric into a smooth curve by gently pushing and pulling it with the point of the needle. (A wooden toothpick also works well, as described on page 81.) Remove the pin as you pass it, and ease the seam allowance under as you approach the next pin. In this way, the pins do the major work for you, allowing you to concentrate on easing and adjusting the tiny humps of fabric rather than struggling with big mounds of fabric.

Stitching Inside Points

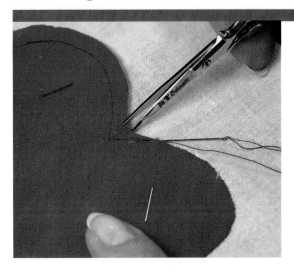

1

When you approach an inside point, such as at the top of a heart, you can stitch no farther until you cut into the seam allowance. For an inside point, it's time to clip into the point when you can no longer turn and ease the seam allowance under easily. **Clip one cut just to the seam line.** Pin on the opposite side as close to the clipped point as you can to hold the loose fabric in place while you sew toward the point.

Tip

Never clip into the seam allowance until you absolutely have to, and then sew the clipped area under immediately.

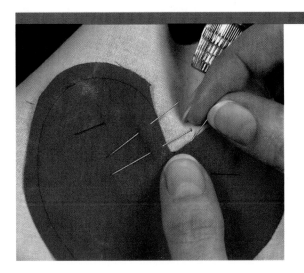

2

Don't think about the other side of the inside point yet. It is anchored and waiting for you. Turn the shape so you are sewing at a comfortable angle. **Use the side of the needle or a toothpick to roll the right side of the seam allowance under. In one motion (if possible), start at the end of the clip and push the needle to the right, easing the seam allowance with it.** Then sew to the point, using your tiniest stitches. To secure the delicate point, take several tiny stitches.

Tip

If your fabric frays easily, swipe a toothpick across a glue stick and use it to sweep under the clipped seam allowance. The glue tames loose threads.

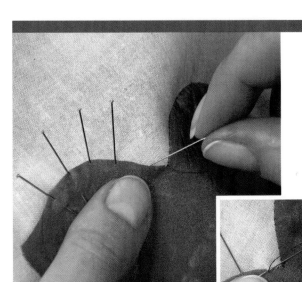

3

Once one side of the inner point is secure, you're ready to move on to the next side. If you have a major curve coming up, such as in our heart example, it's best to pin the curve as described in Step 3 on the opposite page. Then, remove the pin immediately to the left side of the point. **Roll the seam allowance under with the side of the needle and crease the fold with your thumbnail. Sew in tiny stitches, easing the seam allowance as it curves toward the top of the heart.**

Stitching Outside Points

1

As you approach an outside point, such as at the bottom of a heart, stitch all the way to the point. Take a double stitch at the point to anchor it. **A flap of seam allowance fabric will usually be sticking out, depending on the angle of the point.** The narrower the angle, the more fabric will stick out. Finger press the point.

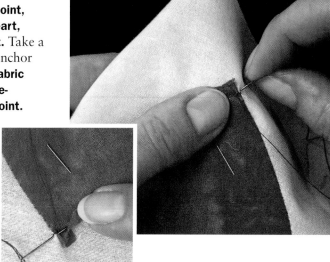

2

Usually you will want to clip away the excess fabric under the point. This will be necessary on the very long narrow point of a leaf, for example. **To do this, turn the appliqué so the point is toward you. Lift the fabric so you can see the flap. Clip just the tail that sticks out beyond the seam allowance.** Be careful not to clip too close to the already sewn point. You need to leave enough fabric to turn under.

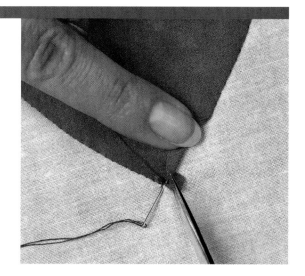

3

With the outside point pointing toward you, hold your hand and the needle toward the point, and use the point of the needle to grab the center of the flap (not the edge, which may fray), and pull it away from you and under the appliqué. Once the point is turned under, adjust the fabric with the needle until it's smooth. Finger press. **Take one longer stitch exactly at the point to secure it.** Pull the thread tight. Continue appliquéing as usual.

The Quilter's
Problem Solver

Pesky Points

Problem	Solution
Outer points aren't sharp. They feel lumpy.	Trim away more of the excess fabric to get a more defined point. The skinnier the outer point, the narrower your seam allowance needs to be. Also, tug on the stitch at the very tip of the point to pull the fabric out and make a crisp, sharp point.
Thread frays on inside points.	Needle turn the fabric in one sideways sweep. If a thread remains visible, use your needle to push it under the already turned seam allowance. Sew it down immediately. For extra security, dab a drop of liquid fabric glue or a dab of glue stick on the outside of the seam allowance before turning it under.

Skill Builder

Here are some additional pointers that are easy to do and can really improve your appliqué proficiency.

❏ Turn your appliqué frequently so that you're always working in a position that's comfortable for you.

❏ Work on background units that are small so you can easily turn them without disrupting your pin-basted pieces. Appliquéing on a full-size quilt background is challenging at best.

❏ If you find it difficult to take the tiny stitches necessary to hold the seam allowance under, particularly on the second side of inside and outside points, try sewing in regular stitches out to about ¼ inch past the point. Then turn and stitch back over your stitches in the opposite direction. This is an easy way to secure the area with many stitches.

Try This!

If your curved edges are bumpy rather than smooth after stitching, you can easily improve the situation. Here are three of the most common pitfalls and easy ways to correct them to improve your results.

❏ Seam allowances may be too wide. Trim them to ⅛ inch or even less.

❏ Stitch tension may be too loose. Pull a bit tighter as you sew, but not so tight as to gather the appliqué.

❏ Stitches may be too far apart. Try to make smaller stitches so the gap between stitches won't be so large.

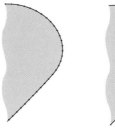

Freezer paper has moved from the kitchen and into the sewing basket, where it has revolutionized hand appliqué. The paper gives support to your appliqué fabric while you stitch, and it keeps your appliqué pieces consistent when shapes are repeated. Best of all, it builds your confidence—your appliqués will be precise and smooth. So even if you never intend to freeze meat, buy a box of freezer paper and try it for appliqué!

Getting Ready

Freezer paper is readily available in many quilt shops or on your grocery shelf near the plastic wrap. Some quilt shops offer it in sheets, and some even have graph paper printed on the uncoated side. If you plan to do a lot of freezer paper appliqué, the 100-square-foot roll may be the way to go.

Refer to "Preparing Shapes for Hand Appliqué" on page 66 for directions about making freezer paper templates and using them to get your fabric pieces ready. Once your shapes are prepared, you'll be ready to jump right in and start stitching. In this chapter, you'll find directions for stitching with freezer paper on the bottom and with freezer paper on the top. They each have their benefits, so you may want to try both methods before deciding on the final method for your project.

What You'll Need

Sequin pins

Freezer paper appliqué shapes

Appliqué fabrics

Background fabric

Silk or appliqué pins

Appliqué needle to match appliqué fabric

Thread to match appliqué fabric

Embroidery scissors or thread snips

Tweezers

Freezer Paper on the Bottom

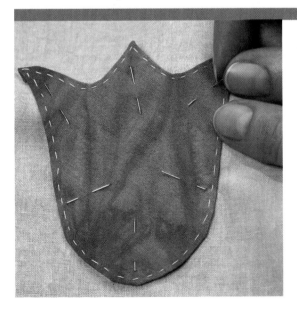

Using ¾-inch straight pins (also called sequin pins), pin the first appliqué piece to the background fabric. Use enough pins to hold the appliqué securely in place. Pin just one appliqué at a time in place for sewing. If your design has pieces that will be layered or overlapped, see "Placing & Layering Appliqué Shapes" on page 22 for details.

Tip

Pin only one appliqué, and stitch it before pinning another. It's easier to maneuver the block, and you won't get stuck on excess pins.

2

Stitch the appliqué in place, using the traditional appliqué stitch. (See "The Perfect Hand Appliqué Stitch" on page 78.) **Your needle should go through the folded edge of the fabric but not through the freezer paper.** If the fabric is not turned tightly over the edge of the paper, move your needle under the appliqué to grab the fabric and pull it taut so that it is smooth along the edge of the paper.

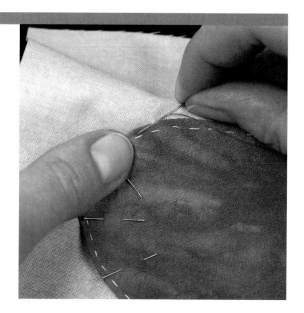

3

After stitching the appliqué in place, remove any basting stitches, using embroidery scissors or thread snips to clip the threads. This is a very important step—the freezer paper won't come out if the basting stitches are holding it inside the fabric.

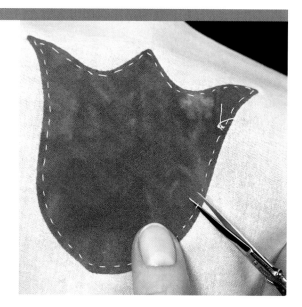

4

One way to remove the paper is from the top. Stop stitching about ¾ inch from where you began your appliqué stitches, and remove the freezer paper from the opening. Before doing so, finger press the edge of the appliqué so it keeps its shape. **Then pull out the basting stitches and freezer paper with tweezers, and finish appliquéing the shape.**

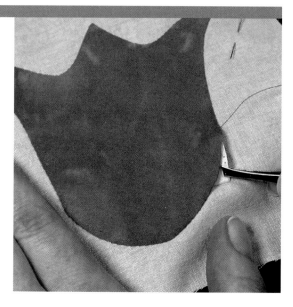

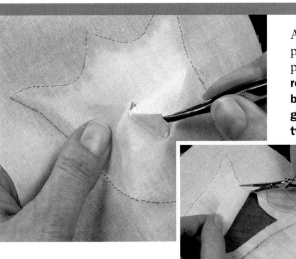

Another way to remove the freezer paper is to completely stitch the appliqué to the background fabric. **Then remove the paper from the wrong side by making a small cut in the background fabric behind the appliqué. Use tweezers to remove the freezer paper.**

Do not sew the cut edges together—this will create a ridge under the appliqué.

If you plan to quilt on top of the appliqué, trim away the background fabric behind the appliqué, leaving ¼-inch seam allowances around the appliqué.

Tip

Cut the background fabric on the bias. The cut will stretch to open but won't fray. After removing the paper, "pet" the cut, smoothing it closed.

Freezer Paper on the Top

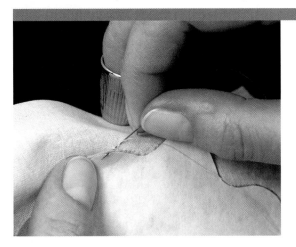

To stitch the appliqué in place with freezer paper on top, simply needle turn the fabric under the paper! Let a small fold of fabric show beyond the edge of the paper for perfect placement of your appliqué stitches. The stitching technique is identical to that shown on pages 79–82. You simply use the paper as the guideline for turning under the edges, rather than following a marked line. So why use paper? It gives the added benefit of stabilizing the shape while you hold it.

When you have completed stitching the appliqué to the background fabric, gently peel off the freezer paper, and press the appliqué. As you can see, the advantage to this method is that you don't have to cut your background fabric or remove the paper before stitching is complete. However, you can still cut away the excess background fabric if you want. Just remember, there's no protective layer of freezer paper between the background and appliqué fabrics, **so be careful when you make a slit in the background fabric.**

Tip

Gently pull the appliqué away from the background so you are sure not to cut into it when you cut away the background fabric.

FREEZER PAPER APPLIQUÉ

Graceful stems and vines, those staples of appliqué design, can be created using several different methods. Bias tubes are the classic technique. But if you have a bias against using bias tubes, these curved elements, and even basket handles, are still within your grasp. Using needle-turn or freezer paper techniques, you can appliqué even the thinnest possible curving stems from a single layer of fabric. This type of stem or vine will be nice and flat, without the added bulk of folded or sewn bias tubes.

Getting Ready

Unlike traditional bias tubes, you won't be cutting your selected fabric into uniform strips across the diagonal grain. Instead, you'll need to plan the shapes of your curves and make templates for them, either from template plastic or freezer paper. (Remember, if you use freezer paper on the bottom, your finished vine will twist in the opposite direction of your drawn template. See page 90 for complete details on making and using freezer paper templates.) A quilter's flexicurve comes in handy for this task. You can form it to any shape or size curve you want, then trace along its edges for smooth lines.

For the most realistic stems or vines that mimic nature, select fabrics that are mottled or slightly patterned.

You can, of course, make bias tubes and hand appliqué them in place. If you prefer that method, see "Bias Stems, Vines & Basket Handles" on page 46 for directions on making accurate bias tubes. Instead of attaching the tubes by machine, you can stitch them in place by hand.

What You'll Need

- **Appliqué pattern**
- **Freezer paper**
- **Quilter's flexicurve**
- **Pencil or Pigma pen**
- **Iron and ironing board**
- **Appliqué fabrics**
- **Fabric scissors**
- **Silk pins or appliqué pins**
- **Threads to match appliqué fabrics**
- **Appliqué needle of choice**
- **Background fabric**
- **Template plastic**
- **Paper or craft scissors**

Freezer Paper Vines

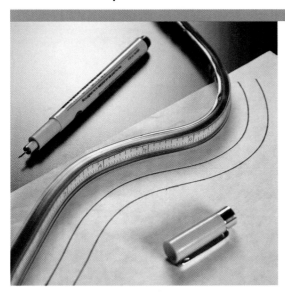

To make a freezer paper template for stems or vines, you can trace the design from a printed appliqué pattern onto freezer paper, or you can create your own curve by shaping a quilter's flexicurve as desired. **Lay the flexicurve on the freezer paper and draw along the edge using a pencil or Pigma pen.** You can trace on both sides of the flexicurve, or, if the flexicurve is wider than you want your vine to be, you can reposition the curve before marking the second side. This will let you make a narrower shape. Cut out the freezer paper vine exactly on the drawn lines.

1

2

Tip

You can position the freezer paper in any direction on the fabric. Grain line isn't critical, since the paper stabilizes the narrow fabric.

With a hot, dry iron, press the freezer paper template to the right side of the vine fabric. Cut out the fabric vine, cutting a scant ¼ inch away from the paper edges. Leave the freezer paper attached to the fabric, where it will act as the turn-under guide for needle-turn appliqué.

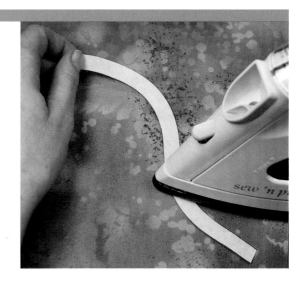

3

Tip

If the freezer paper should start to lift from the fabric as you are stitching, simply use a hot iron to re-adhere it to the fabric.

Pin the appliqué vine to the background fabric, matching the marked guidelines if you have them. **Beginning at one end of the vine, turn under the raw edge even with the freezer paper and stitch.** (See "The Perfect Hand Appliqué Stitch" on page 78 for more details.)

When you reach the end of one side of the vine, end the stitching. Do not turn under the end of the vine. That should remain flat where it will be covered by another appliqué element. **Restart your stitching along the opposite side of the vine, again leaving the other end of the vine flat and unstitched.**

Needle-Turn Vines & Handles

1

Although the freezer paper can help stabilize the vines as you stitch, some people prefer to use needle-turn appliqué without the paper. In this case, trace the vine onto template plastic from the printed pattern, or draw your own shape using a flexicurve. **Cut out the template exactly on the drawn lines.**

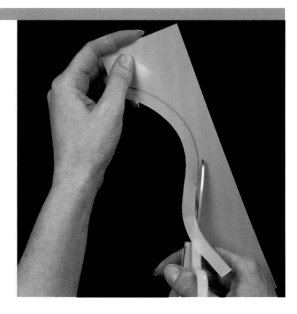

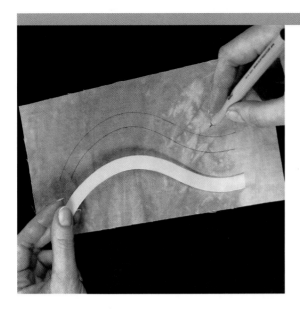

Lay the plastic template on the right side of the vine fabric, and draw around it using a quilter's silver pencil or a Pigma pen. Cut out the vine a scant ¼ inch outside the drawn lines. Pin or baste the vine in place.

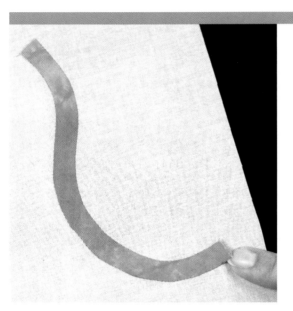

Stitch the vine in place by turning under the edge directly on the marked line as you stitch. **As with the freezer paper method, do not turn under the ends of the vine.** They should be left flat to lie smoothly under appliqué shapes that will be added later.

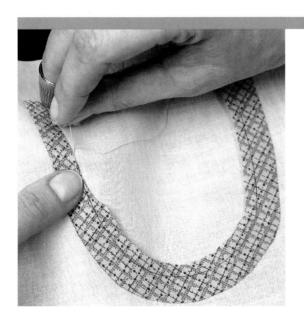

Basket handles can be made in exactly the same way. Instead of having to bend bias tubes into a handle shape, make a template of the exact shape you want your basket handle to be, and cut out the fabric as described above. **Notice that when you are appliquéing the handle, it doesn't matter if you stitch the inside or outside edge first, since you don't have to worry about easing in or stretching bias to fit the curve.** This type of handle will lie perfectly flat because it isn't bent to form a curve.

Tip

Plaids make great basket handles, especially when the template is placed on the bias.

STEMS & VINES BY HAND

 riginally, folk art was a spontaneous outpouring of creativity from people who didn't have any formal training. Early folk-style quilts had appliqués that were neither perfectly shaped nor sophisticated—but nonetheless, these quilts had a whimsical charm. Today, greater appreciation and respect have been lavished on early folk quilts, with their quirky flowers, hearts, animals, and primitive stitches. It is easy to see why these delightful quilts are so well loved. For today's busy quilters, there's another very endearing charm to folk art appliqué—it's fast!

Getting Ready

You can become part of the folk art tradition by stitching your own quilt using wool, cotton, flannel, or felt, using either a purchased pattern or a design you created yourself. Folk art appliqué has a casual look, but it pays to plan ahead so the mood of the piece is just right. Decide on the design and color scheme you want. Consider how the piece will be displayed—as a wall hanging or a table runner, perhaps. How much use will it get, and how will it be handled? Then choose the fabric, draft your templates, and mark and cut the fabric pieces. If you select wool or felt, you simply need to cut out the shapes without seam allowances. If you want to use cotton with turned-under seam allowances, see page 66 for details. All of the methods below can be used on a variety of fabrics, and each will change the piece in subtle ways.

If you like the look of folk art appliqué but prefer machine appliqué, see "The Stitch Sampler" on page 32 for directions on doing blanket stitch appliqué by machine.

What You'll Need

Fabrics: wool, cotton, flannel, or felt

Appliqué patterns

Threads: embroidery floss, perle cotton, wool yarn, Burmiliana, buttonhole, quilting, or linen

Large-eye embroidery needles

Silk or appliqué pins

Thread snips or embroidery scissors

Fusible web or water-soluble glue stick

Folk Art Appliqué

1

Use wool, flannel, felt (as was used in old penny rugs), and homespun-looking cotton fabric, especially checks and plaids, to achieve a folk art feeling in your quilt. Fabrics that look old will look great, too, so if you prefer cotton, look for some of the many period reproduction fabrics currently available. Black and mud brown are traditional background colors. Appliqués can be any color, although heathery, muted colors replicate the look of old, hand-dyed fabrics. On the other hand, the Pennsylvania Dutch colors—bright, clear reds, greens, blues, and yellows—show that the range of folk colors is unlimited.

2

Old-time folk quilts were not elegant. The shapes in appliqué designs were neither perfect nor formally arranged. They were simple and crude, perhaps a little lopsided and childlike. **The traditional elements we see in folk quilts of the past are hearts, hands, stars, simplified animal silhouettes, patriotic eagles, and simple flowers and leaves.** Any shape is acceptable, of course, as long as you can hold yourself back from perfection and allow a little whimsy to enter your designs.

3

There are many thread choices for folk quilts, and your choice may depend upon the type of fabric you use. For wool or felt appliqués, it's fun to use embroidery floss, size 5 perle cotton, a fine wool yarn, or Burmiliana. They're showy when used in decorative hand appliqué stitches. For cotton appliqués, try buttonhole thread, quilting thread, linen thread, or a lighter-weight perle cotton (size 8).

Black thread against any color is traditional, but if you want the thread to show, use a color that contrasts with the fabric so the thread stands out.

Tip

For a more subtle folk look, use thread that's the same color as the appliqué, but a shade or two darker.

4

When you use a bulkier thread, you'll need to change the type of needle you use. **Embroidery needles have larger eyes, but they are still long and sharp enough for appliqué.** To thread a multi-strand thread or floss, you may find it easier if you fold the end of the thread over the needle and pull both ends taut with your left hand. Then slip the needle out of thread while your other hand continues to pinch the fold tight. **Slip the fold through the needle's eye.**

Unlike elegant appliqué, where the goal is to hide the stitches, one of the charms of folk appliqué is that you want the stitches to show. One fun way to do this is with a running stitch. Pin a prepared appliqué shape (either with freezer paper or basted edges) to the background. **Using a running stitch, stitch just inside the folded seam edge by simply lacing the needle through from top to bottom and back up again.** Try to make stitches roughly the same length on the top of the fabric as they are on the bottom. Stitches can be large and crude or small and fine.

For appliqués prepared with turned-under edges and freezer paper, use a sharp embroidery needle to penetrate the layers of fabric and paper.

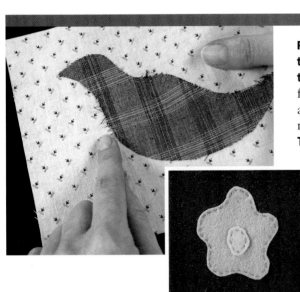

For an even more primitive look, use the running stitch on cotton without turning the edges under. Cotton will fray with time and give the appliqué a used look. Woven plaid fabrics make great choices for this method. **The running stitch also works nicely on felt or felted wool.** Do not turn under edges. These fabrics are bulky and the edges won't fray, so leaving them unturned is best. Because wool and felt are thicker, it's not as easy to maneuver the needle in and out once you have a few stitches on the needle. Simply take one stitch at a time through these fabrics.

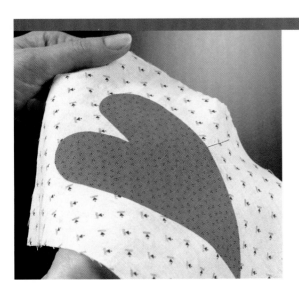

The blanket stitch is often seen on primitive appliqué. It's fun and easy to do around shapes that don't need seam allowances, such as felt or wool appliqués or cotton appliqués that are prepared with fusible web. (See page 31 for directions on making fusible shapes.) If you're not using fusible web, anchor the shape in place on the background with either pins or a dab of glue. **Insert your needle from the back of the work so it comes out through the background fabric only, just at the edge of the appliqué shape.**

To anchor a shape with glue, dab it in the center only. Avoid edges because glue hardens, making it impossible to sew through.

8

Hold the thread to the left of where it came through the background fabric. **Insert the tip of the needle in the appliqué about ¼ inch to the left of where it came up and about ¼ inch deep into the edge of the fabric. Bring the tip of the needle back up at the edge of the appliqué, so it is in front of the thread you are holding tautly in your left hand.** Pull the thread all the way through the fabric to complete the stitch. **Continue making blanket stitches in the same manner all the way around your shape.**

9

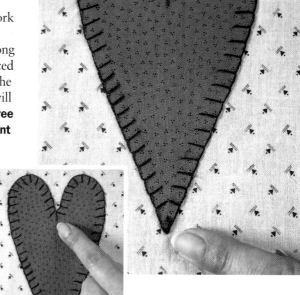

You will need to adjust spacing to work blanket stitches around points. At outer points, the stitches that run along the edge of the shape should be spaced about the same distance apart, but the stitches that bite into the appliqué will be very close together. **Notice that three stitches—one on each side of the point and the one directly at the point—all start near the same place.**

For inside points, the stitches on the appliqué are splayed apart. The important thing is to take a stitch directly at the point itself, whether it is an inside or outside point.

10

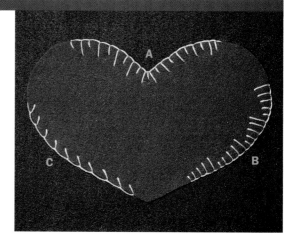

You can enhance the humble blanket stitch by making simple variations. Varying the length of your stitches is an easy way to change the look (A). Other options include an ascending set of five stitches (B), which looks elegant. Or try sewing the stitches at an angle to resemble the feathers of an arrow (C).

The Quilter's
Problem Solver

Thread Troubles

Problem	Solution
Multistrand thread tangles.	After threading the needle, run the length of thread over a block of beeswax. Your thread will be much easier to control. Scrape off excess wax with your thumbnail, or press it with your iron. (Put a paper towel on your ironing board to protect it from the melted wax.)
Which is best—floss or perle cotton?	The answer really depends on the look you want. Floss is often more readily available in a large number of colors. You can use any number of threads from the skein of embroidery floss for stitching. Three strands of floss make a modest contrast against the fabric, while the full six is dramatic. Perle cotton, on the other hand, is a twisted thread and retains a nice rounded shape as it sits on the fabric surface. It is not separated into strands. Try different thicknesses for different effects. Size 3 is has a nice bulky look; size 5 works better for felt and wool; and size 8 is thinner and works well for flannels and cottons.

Skill Builder

Folk art lends itself to simple, free-form designs. It is the perfect place to try your hand at original design. Try cutting paper shapes of animals, flowers, or other objects for patterns. Remember to keep your designs simple, easy to cut, and easy to stitch around—nothing so narrow or delicate that you won't have room for a blanket or running stitch around all the edges. Place your shapes in a pleasing arrangement and stitch them down. Finish the practice piece as a table runner or pillow so you can use and enjoy it. You will learn from all aspects of the design process without the stress of having to create something grand, elegant, and perfect.

Try This!

The feather stitch is another traditional folk appliqué stitch, and it gives variety and direction to appliqué elements. It, too, is worked easily on fabrics without seam allowances, such as felt or wool. Anchor the shape in place on the background with either pins or glue. Choose the direction to sew. On a heart, it is fun to have the feathers flow down the two sides from the top, as shown. The feathery side stitches can extend at acute or relaxed angles and be long or short. Experiment to find the appropriate look for your project.

FOLK ART HAND APPLIQUÉ

103

Dimensional Appliqué

Once you've mastered the basics of appliqué, there's nothing to stop you from taking your appliqué skills into another whole dimension. Three-dimensional appliqué is often a feature of album-style quilts, and it has gained real popularity with the resurgence of interest in Baltimore-album quilts. First of all, 3-D elements are fun to make. Plus, the gently bending flower petals, puffed flower centers, dainty rosebuds, and sculpted leaves make you want to reach right out and touch—or smell—a quilt.

Getting Ready

Before beginning, gather together some of your favorite appliqué patterns. As you read this chapter, refer to the patterns often to see which design elements could be replaced by pieces made from one of the dimensional techniques described in this chapter. For instance, a ruched blossom could be substituted for a rose with many individual pieces. Gathered leaves could replace flat ones.

Most of the techniques in this chapter require only small pieces of fabric. However, for one method, called ruching, you'll need to use long, crosswise-grain strips.

Although dimensional appliqué is often seen in floral designs, consider using the techniques in this chapter for other types of blocks, too. Gathering and folding techniques can add depth and realism to any quilt.

What You'll Need

Template plastic or oak tag

Rotary-cutting supplies

Paper or craft scissors

Pencil or fine-point permanent marker

Appliqué fabrics

Sewing machine

Iron and ironing board

Appliqué needles of choice

Threads to match appliqué fabrics

Thread snips or embroidery scissors

Silk or appliqué pins

Background fabric

Protractor, compass, or other circle-drawing tool

Fabric scissors

Freezer paper

Ruching

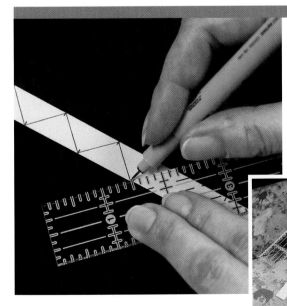

Ruching is a simple gathering technique that makes it easy to construct textured flowers, vines, basket handles, and a variety of other shapes for your appliqué quilt. To make a ruching guide, cut a strip of template material ½ × 8 inches. Beginning at the left end, make marks along the top edge, exactly 1 inch apart. Make a second set of marks along the lower edge, spacing them halfway between the upper marks. **Connect the upper and lower marks with straight lines to form a zigzag pattern.**

Durable, die-cut ruching guides can be purchased at quilt shops if you'd rather not make your own guide.

1

Tip

Try working with bias strips, too, to see which type of grain line is easiest for you to gather and fold for your desired effects.

2

Cut a straight-grain strip of fabric 1¾ inches wide and approximately 30 inches long. Fold the strip lengthwise, with right sides together. Use a short machine stitch and a ¼-inch seam allowance to sew the long edge together. Trim back the seam allowance to slightly less than ⅛ inch. **Turn the tube right side out and press, centering the seam in the middle of the reverse side.**

3

Position the pressed strip right side up under the ruching guide, aligning their left edges. **Use a pencil or other marker to place dots on both folded edges of the strip—matching the marks on the guide.** Move the guide along the strip until you have marked the entire length. If you prefer, you can use a ruler and marker to connect the dots on the fabric to create a sewing guide. However, mark lightly or use a removable marker, since marks can show after ruching is complete. You can just as easily stitch from dot to dot, without marking a line.

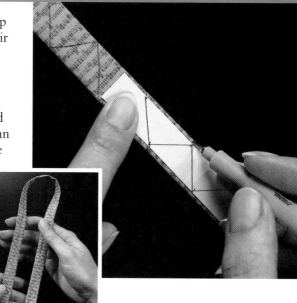

Tip

Because you'll be tugging and gathering layers of fabric, it's helpful to use quilting thread for ruching since it's stronger.

4

To gather the strip, hand sew a running stitch between the dots. Bring your needle up through the fold at the first mark on the beginning end of the strip. Take a few small stitches to secure the thread, then sew a gathering stitch between the dots, moving from the top to the bottom edge in the same zigzag pattern you marked on the guide. When you reach the bottom, end with the needle and thread on the back side. Then bring the needle up and over the folded edge when you change direction. Note: Use matching thread. We used contrasting thread so you could see it.

After you've stitched 6 to 8 inches, pull the thread to gather the fabric, forming petal-like scallops on each side of the strip. Use your fingers to adjust the scallops if necessary. Continue sewing and gathering until you've achieved the desired length. The gathered strip can be used just as it is for vines, stems, cattails, basket handles, and other similar pieces.

Tip

To make vinelike shapes, begin with strips that are approximately twice as long as the finished length of the appliqué piece.

6

Add security to the gathers by machine sewing a short stitch across threads at each end of the desired length. Place the strip right side up on the quilt, then baste it in place or secure with pins. Tuck raw edges under overlapping pieces, or if they won't be covered by another piece, fold the ends under. Appliqué in place with matching thread.

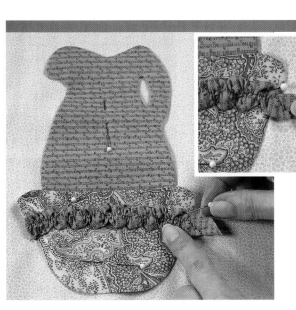

7

To make gathered flowers, turn under the raw edge at the first scallop or petal, and hand stitch it in place. Twist the first five or six petals to form a circle, then take a stitch through their centers to bring them together to form a blossom center. **Add a new round of petals by winding the strip behind the first round.** Tack the petals in the new round to petals in the first. **Continue adding rounds until the flower is the desired size.** Smooth the last petal into place, and tuck its raw edges under the previous row. Tack the raw edge to secure.

Tip

For smaller, more closely spaced scallops, make a ruching guide with points spaced ½" apart.

D I M E N S I O N A L   A P P L I Q U É

8

Beginning at the outer edge, hand appliqué the ruched flower to the background fabric, taking stitches through each outside petal at its center and inside points.

To embellish the blossom, use beads, a small button, or French knots to add stamens at the center of the flower, placing them slightly off center for a more realistic look.

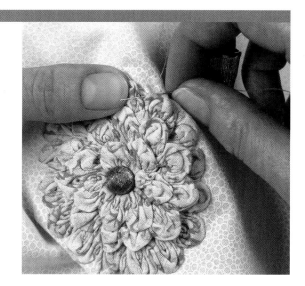

Folded Blossoms from Circles

1

Tip

To make a straight fold, position a bias bar in the fold so that the fabric meets the center point when folded tautly over the bar. Press.

It's quick and easy to make three-dimensional flower blossoms from fabric circles. Use a protractor or compass to draw a 4-inch-diameter circle on one fabric and a 2-inch-diameter circle on a contrasting fabric. Cut out both circles and mark the center point of each on the wrong side of the fabric. **Beginning with the larger circle, fold one side in to meet the center mark. Press or finger press the fold,** and secure the edge with a pin.

2

Tip

For more ideas on folding fabrics, browse through an origami book. You'll find many designs that can be adapted for use in appliqué.

Fold the next edge toward the center point so that the point where the creased edge of the first fold meets the curve of the circle is folded to meet the center point exactly. Press and pin. **Continue working around the circle, making a total of six equal folds.** Tack the blossom at the center to hold folds in place. Prepare the smaller circle in the same way, then center and appliqué it to the larger folded unit. Add a button, if you wish. Appliqué the finished blossom to the quilt.

To make a folded bud, cut a circle and fold it in half. **Then fold the semi-circle into thirds by folding in one-third starting at the midpoint of the straight edge.** Fold in the other side to overlap. Pin in place.

Hand stitch a running stitch along the bottom edge of the circle, and pull to gather the bud. Secure the gather by taking several small stitches. Place the gathered edge under the calyx of the flower on the appliqué pattern.

Tip

To replace a "flat" bud, measure the length of the pattern, multiply it by 2, and then add ½" for seam allowances. The result is the diameter of the circle to cut.

Gathered Partial Leaves

This technique adds depth to partial leaves (leaves that are partially hidden behind blossoms, vines, or other leaves). Cut out a freezer paper template of the partial leaf pattern. **Cut a slit in the freezer paper template from the midpoint of the leaf base to near the leaf's tip. Spread the slit approximately ⅜ inch apart at its base, and press it onto the fabric.**

Cut out the leaf, adding a scant ¼-inch seam allowance to all sides as you cut. Turn under the seam allowances on leaf sides, and baste or glue in place. (See page 16 for directions on preparing edges of shapes.)

Hand sew a gathering stitch near the edge of the base, securing the starting point with a backstitch. Gather the stitches until the base is the same width as the original printed pattern. Backstitch to secure the gathering thread. **Tuck the base edge under a stem or flower and appliqué the leaf to the background.**

Tip

You can add dimension to flower buds and other shapes by gathering their bases in the same manner.

D I M E N S I O N A L   A P P L I Q U É

Layered Mock Yo-Yos

1

Cut a 2 × 5-inch strip of fabric and a 1 × 5-inch strip of a contrasting fabric. With right sides facing, sew the fabrics together lengthwise, and trim the seam allowance to slightly less than ⅛ inch. Press the seam open. **Fold under approximately ³⁄₁₆ inch on each long edge, wrong sides facing. Press to secure the fold.**

2

Fold the pieced strip in half crosswise with right sides together. **Sew a seam along the short unfolded edge, then trim the seam allowance to slightly less than ⅛ inch.** Press the seam open, and turn the tube right side out. If you find it difficult to press open such a narrow seam, you can press it open first, then trim each side to ⅛ inch.

3

Tip

Use slightly longer or shorter strip lengths to make larger or smaller blossoms.

Hand sew a gathering seam through the folds on both open edges of the tube, backstitching at each starting point to secure the thread. **Pull the thread on one edge, gathering the tube into a compact circle.** Backstitch and knot to secure the thread.

Gather the remaining edge, backstitch, and knot. **Press the centers together to form the blossom.** Appliqué to the quilt with the narrower, contrasting edge on top.

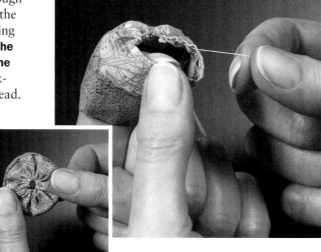

110

The Quilter's
Problem Solver

Breaking Threads & Problem Pins

Problem	Solution
Thread keeps breaking when gathering ruffles.	Try sewing the gathering stitches with quilting thread, which is stronger than regular sewing thread. Another good choice is nylon beading thread. Or, if you use regular sewing thread, you can use it doubled.
Thread constantly catches on pins when appliquéing pieces to the background.	Place enough pins through the front of pieces to secure them to the background, then flip the block over and do a thorough pinning from the back. Remove the front pins to eliminate thread snags. To eliminate pin pricks to your hands or lap, bury the pin tips in the fabric.
You're beginning to work on a project that has been put away for awhile, and you can't figure out which piece goes where.	When you store pieces for any project, place like patches or patches that will be sewn near each other in plastic sandwich bags. Label the bag in any way that will help you decipher its contents the next time you work on the quilt.

Skill Builder

Imitate nature with your fabric selections. Even though they sometimes appear to be composed of a single, solid color, most flowers, plants, animals, insects, landscapes—and nearly every other item we see in nature—is a blend of many shades. You can achieve a mottled appearance in your dimensional appliqué by selecting fabrics that contain more than one shade of a single color. Mottled prints and hand-dyed fabrics are great choices. When gathered together, the shading adds depth and more visual interest than a single color. Look to nature for ways to mix colors, too. You'll likely discover many combinations you hadn't considered in the past.

Try This!

Don't limit yourself to using cotton fabric for dimensional appliqué. Ruching and gathering techniques are lovely when applied to French wired ribbons, and the result is a variety of elegant florals to decorate quilts and other items such as totes, hats, and clothing. Although French ribbons often appear fragile, most are washable. Just be sure to check labels for care instructions.

❑ To gather wired ribbon along an edge, hold the wire with one hand while you push the ribbon along its length.

❑ There's no need to fold or baste wired ribbons before ruching; just stitch the zigzag line between the finished outer edges. Gathering stitches for ruched ribbons can vary in length. Experiment to see how stitch length affects the gathers.

DIMENSIONAL APPLIQUÉ

Reverse
Appliqué

S hift into reverse for some very special appliqué. Instead of adding appliqué shapes to the top of the background fabric, you can trim away the top layer of fabric and stitch the edges in place to let the lower fabric peek through. Reverse appliqué is also an innovative way to add lovely layered effects in flowers, leaves, and other designs that you will be appliquéing to a background fabric. While not quite as bold as dimensional appliqué, reverse-appliquéd shapes let you play with color and shading combinations in a whole new way.

Getting Ready

Examine your appliqué pattern to determine if it's a good candidate for reverse appliqué. The primary benefit of reverse appliqué is that outer, or *convex*, curves in regular appliqué become inner, or *concave*, curves in reverse appliqué, and these are easier to stitch. For example, when stitching a heart by needle-turn appliqué, you need to turn under the seam allowance and fit the fabric of the seam allowance underneath the outer curves of the heart. If you appliqué that same heart shape by reverse appliqué, however, you'll be working with a concave curve—that of the top fabric, surrounding the heart shape. This means that the finished appliqué will lie flatter, without bunching. While reverse appliqué isn't suitable for every occasion, you'll find it extremely helpful when stitching inside lots of small, curved pieces, especially on a shape like a feathered heart.

Note: Always use matching thread. We used white thread so it shows clearly in the photographs.

Reverse Appliqué

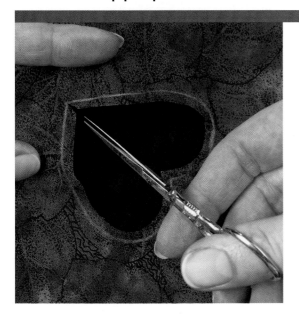

1

Mark your appliqué design on the top layer of fabric. Cut a seam allowance approximately 3/16 inch *inside* the marked lines of the reverse appliqué shape, which in this example is a heart. **Using a small, sharp pair of embroidery scissors, clip up to (but not *through*) the marked turning line at inner points on the appliqué, such as the lower point of the heart.**

2

Pin the top fabric in position on your square of contrasting center fabric. **Make clips into the seam allowance along any inner curves on the appliqué, spacing them approximately ³⁄₁₆ to ¼ inch apart.** Take care not to cut through the marked turning line as you work your way around the shape. These clips will make it easy to smoothly turn the fabric under along the curves as you stitch.

3

Tip

For best results, always begin stitching on straight or gently curved areas rather than on deep inner or outer curves and points.

To hide the knotted thread, hold the contrasting center fabric and the top fabric between your thumb and middle finger, and **bring the threaded needle up through the top fabric only, just *outside* the marked turning line.** Use the tip of a wooden toothpick to turn the edge of the fabric under gently, so that the marked turning line is just out of sight. **Crease the fold slightly with your left thumbnail,** and stitch to approximately ⅛ inch from the point. (See "The Perfect Hand Appliqué Stitch" on page 78 for more details.)

4

To create sharp inner points, run the tip of a toothpick over a water-soluble glue stick, and use it to turn under any exposed thread or threads at the point. Gently pinch the top fabric to the background fabric to make sure the threads stay securely in place, and then stitch all the way to the lower point. **Take one reinforcing stitch to anchor the lower point.**

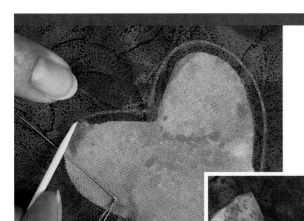

Rotate your work and continue stitching, using a toothpick to turn under the seam allowance gently, approximately ¼ inch at a time. Lightly finger crease the fold with your left thumbnail before stitching this distance. **Continue working your way around the shape in this manner.**

For outside points like the top of a heart, stitch one side of the point completely, right up to the marked point. Next, use the tip of the toothpick to turn under the seam allowance on the unstitched side of the point. **Then tug gently on the thread, pulling the fabric out into a sharp point.** Take one slightly longer stitch that goes straight out from the point into the background fabric approximately $\frac{1}{32}$ inch. **This little "fool-the-eye" stitch will enhance the point, making it look razor sharp.**

Tip

If there is too much bulk at an outer point, trim the seam allowance underneath slightly before stitching the next side.

Continue stitching around the shape, folding under ¼ inch at a time, and space your final stitch an even distance from your first one. After you have ended and clipped the thread, place your completed work right side down on top of a terry cloth towel. Spritz the fabric lightly with water, and press it with a hot, dry iron on the cotton setting to give it a crisp, flat finish.

REVERSE APPLIQUÉ

8

To make a reverse appliqué shape that can then be appliquéd onto a background fabric, reverse appliqué a shape, as described above. **Then, using a Pigma pen or quilter's silver pencil, mark a larger shape on the top fabric, *outside* the lines of the finished reverse appliquéd shape.** (The example shows a heart, but you can use this technique on leaves, flowers, or any shape you want.)

9

Trim away the center fabric underneath the stitched area, taking care to trim close to the edge of the turned-under seam allowance. **Then, trim away the remaining top fabric outside the larger heart shape,** so that a 3/16-inch seam allowance remains around the entire shape.

10

Position the trimmed shape on the background fabric. Bring a threaded needle up just inside the marked turning line on one side of the shape, and **appliqué the entire shape as you would normally appliqué any shape.** As you turn under the edges of the top fabric, the edges of the center fabric will be encased. This will complete the layered heart with a contrasting center fabric.

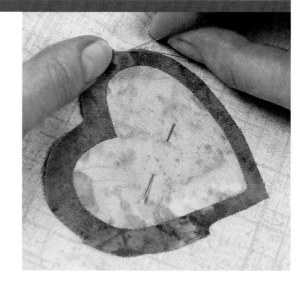

The Quilter's
Problem Solver

Taming the Fabric for Reverse Appliqué

Problem	Solution
I'm not sure how far to clip into a reverse appliqué seam allowance.	Clipping the seam allowance of an inner curve for reverse appliqué is easy, if you remember to stop each clip just *short* of your marked turning line. That way, it's easy to be sure that the outline of the shape will remain smooth and unbroken after it has been stitched.
Trimming away a lower layer of fabric is tricky.	Instead of turning your stitching over and cutting away the lower layer of fabric from the *wrong* side, try working from the *right* side. Simply lift up the top layer of fabric, exposing the turned-under seam allowance. Hold it out of the way while you trim the lower layer of fabric even with the turned-under seam allowance.
Stray threads pop up at inner points.	Just as in needle-turn appliqué, stray threads at inner points can be tamed by a bit of water-soluble glue stick on the tip of a wooden toothpick. Just tuck the tip of the toothpick under at the inner point, and pinch the top fabric to the underneath layer to control the threads. Then take a single reinforcement stitch right at the point before stitching the next side of the reverse appliqué shape.

Skill Builder

Seam allowances make great padding!

For layered reverse appliqué shapes, try trimming away the lower layer of fabric so that it is a bit *wider* than the seam allowance of the top fabric. When you turn under the seam allowance on the top fabric to appliqué it, this small amount of extra fabric in the underneath fabric will fill out the edges and give the completed reverse appliqué shape more loft and added visual dimension.

Try This!

Use reverse appliqué anytime. You don't have to save the technique for special occasions and fancy pieces. While a reverse-appliquéd feathered wreath is breathtaking, reverse appliqué works just as well on more folksy projects. Give an appliquéd chicken a reverse appliquéd wing inside the body shape. Or use an unexpected fabric peeking out between the layers for an element of surprise. Let your imagination go free. You'll soon be thinking of lots of uses for this time-honored technique.

REVERSE APPLIQUÉ

Cutwork
Appliqué

Think of this technique as the "cut as you go" method of appliqué. Instead of precutting the shape, you mark it onto a piece of fabric and cut the seam allowance a bit at a time as you stitch it onto a square of background fabric. Cutwork appliqué is a great way to position long, slender shapes like stems or vines with precision, and it's also helpful for stitching large, intricate designs such as Hawaiian or Tahitian appliqué motifs.

Getting Ready

Whether you're using a purchased pattern or designing your own, take a look at what kind of shapes are involved. Cutwork appliqué is useful for large pieces that are cut entirely from one fabric, such as a Hawaiian appliqué. If you cut out the entire intricate pattern before you start to sew, it would become quite hard to manage without twisting and stretching the design out of shape. But cutwork appliqué has applications beyond Hawaiian appliqué. Appliqué borders—such as swags and dogtooth borders that are also cut from one piece of fabric—become much more manageable when you use the cut-as-you-go technique. Floral sprays, where several intersecting stems meet in the block center, are another good choice for cutwork appliqué. Instead of making each stem from a separate piece of fabric, you can cut them all from one large square—cutting as you go!

What You'll Need

- Appliqué pattern
- Freezer paper
- Pigma pen, size .01, or quilter's silver marking pencil
- Paper or craft scissors
- Appliqué fabrics
- Iron and ironing board
- Background fabric
- Silk or appliqué pins
- Sharp embroidery scissors
- Appliqué needle of choice
- Thread to match appliqué fabrics
- Thimble
- Round wooden toothpick with sharp tip
- Terry cloth towel

Folded Cutwork Patterns

To work with a Hawaiian pattern, you can fold freezer paper into quarters or eighths, and then trace just one quadrant or eighth of the pattern onto the folded freezer paper. When you cut out the design through all layers, the freezer paper template will be symmetrical. Then fold the appliqué fabric in half vertically and horizontally, and lightly finger crease to find the center. Position the freezer paper template at the center of the fabric so that the coated side is against the fabric. Using a dry iron, gently press the template onto the fabric. **Allow the fabric to cool, and use a Pigma pen or a silver pencil to mark around all of the cut edges of the template.**

Tip

To make marking easier, lay the fabric on a rotary cutting mat to stabilize it as you mark around the freezer paper.

119

2

Tip

Freezer paper can be used several times before its plastic coating no longer sticks. Save your template to make other blocks.

Fold the background fabric in half vertically and horizontally, and lightly finger crease to find its center. Peel away the freezer paper from the appliqué fabric, and position the appliqué fabric on the background fabric, matching the centers. **Using silk or appliqué pins, pin the top fabric to the background square at the center and the corners.** If you prefer, you can thread baste rather than pin baste. When working on a large project, such as a full-size Hawaiian appliqué quilt, thread basting may take longer, but it will be much easier to maneuver the quilt without getting stuck.

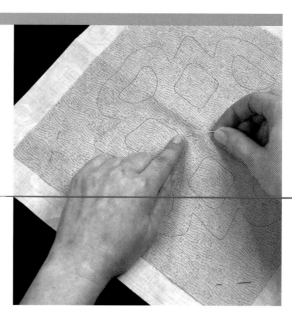

3

Starting with one of the shapes near the center of the design, use a pair of embroidery scissors to clip into the top fabric *only,* and cut a ³⁄₁₆-inch seam allowance *inside* the shape for a distance of approximately 1 inch. By cutting only a small amount at a time the project will remain flat and smooth. Since there are many areas to be cut, the design could stretch and shift if everything were cut out at the beginning.

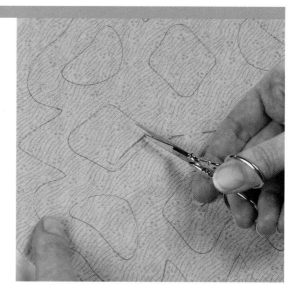

4

Tip

Put a few sequin pins near the area where you stitch to stabilize the top and background fabrics and keep them from shifting.

The shapes inside the pattern will be reverse appliquéd (see page 112). **Bring a threaded needle up just *outside* the marked turning line.** Using the tip of a wooden toothpick, turn under the fabric on the turning line for approximately ¼ to ½ inch. Gently finger crease the fold with your left thumbnail, and appliqué that distance. (See "The Perfect Hand Appliqué Stitch" on page 78 for more details.) Then cut another inch or so of seam allowance, turn it under, finger crease it, and continue stitching. Work your way around each shape in the same way.

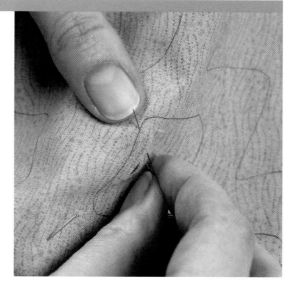

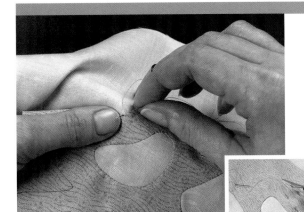

To stitch the outer edges of the pattern, cut into the top fabric *only* at one of the straighter areas. Trim a ³⁄₁₆-inch seam allowance approximately 1 inch long. Bring a threaded needle up just inside your marked turning line, and begin to appliqué the outer edges of the design. **Work your way around the entire design in this manner, cutting, turning, and stitching just a bit of fabric at a time.**

Traced Cutwork Patterns

Of course, cutwork appliqué can be used for patterns other than folded, symmetrical designs. Another popular example is a floral spray-type block, where the stems are narrow and connect to others in the block. To cut out such narrow designs ahead of time would be tricky, as the shapes would tend to bend and stretch out of shape. **Mark the design onto the fabric as with any other needle-turn design (see page 23), but don't cut it out.** You can use either freezer paper or a plastic template to mark your design.

Pin the entire piece of appliqué fabric to the background fabric, as described in Step 3 on the opposite page. **Then, just as in Step 5 above, cut a ³⁄₁₆-inch seam allowance for 1 inch. Appliqué, then cut about another inch-worth of seam allowance.** Continue in this manner until the entire shape is cut and appliquéd.

Tip

Since the background fabric isn't premarked with placement lines, an acetate overlay is helpful for placing other shapes. See page 26.

Appliqué *Glossary*

A

Appliqué. Attaching small pieces of fabric to a background fabric by hand or machine stitching.

Appliqué stitch. An invisible hand stitch used to secure edges of appliqué shapes to the background. Also called a blindstitch.

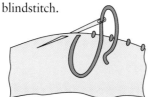

B

Background fabric. The fabric to which appliqué pieces are attached.

Basting. Securing pieces to the background fabric in preparation for sewing. Pieces can be basted in place with a needle and thread using a running stitch or with pins.

Bias press bars. Nylon or metal bars, available in a variety of widths, which are used to make accurate tubes from bias strips of fabric. After stitching a tube, the appropriate-size bar is inserted into the tube before pressing. Finished bias tubes are used to create narrow elements that bend, such as vines, handles, stems, and tendrils. Also called Celtic bars.

Center seam and press flat

Blanket stitch. A hand or machine stitch that results in a series of threads that are parallel to each other. Sometimes called buttonhole stitch, but this is a misnomer, since in the buttonhole stitch the threads are much closer together than in the blanket stitch.

Bobbinfil. A lightweight thread used in the bobbin when doing machine appliqué.

Broderie perse. Appliqué where printed motifs are cut out and appliquéd with a fine blanket stitch to the background.

Buttonhole stitch. A hand stitch sewn in a similar manner to the blanket stitch but with stitches closer together.

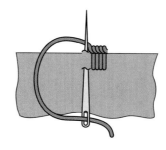

C

Concave curve. A curve that rounds inward, as if a bite were taken out of the piece. Also called inside curve.

Convex curve. A curve that rounds outward, such as the

outside edge of a circle. Also called outside curve.

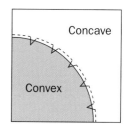
Concave

Convex

Cutwork appliqué. A method where the appliqué shape is marked onto fabric but not cut out. The shape is basted to the background and cut a little at a time as you stitch. This method is particularly suitable for intricate designs, such as Hawaiian appliqué, and curving designs, such as vines, stems, and basket handles.

D

Dimensional appliqué. Appliqué where the pieces rise above the surface of the background fabric. Fabric may be folded, gathered, or stuffed to achieve a three-dimensional look, which is especially popular in album-style quilts.

E

Embroidery floss. A six-ply cotton thread used for folk art appliqué, especially when the appliqués are made of wool or felt. All six strands may be used together, or they may be separated and used two or three at a time for a finer stitch.

Embroidery needle. A hand sewing needle often used for folk art appliqué, since its larger eye accommodates the bulkier threads commonly used for that method.

Embroidery scissors. Short, very sharp scissors with pointed tips.

F

Facing. For appliqué, a facing refers to a shape cut out of interfacing to match the finished size and shape of a pattern piece. The facing is sewn to the right side of the fabric shape, which is then turned right side out. The facing finishes the edges of the appliqué smoothly so they don't need to be turned under and basted in place.

Finger press. Using your fingernail to "press" a temporary crease into a fabric.

Flexicurve. A length of pliable plastic that allows you to mark curves on templates and fabric accurately. A flexicurve is helpful in marking basket handles, vines, stems, and other long, curved shapes.

Folk art appliqué. A whimsical, casual type of appliqué where pieces may not be perfectly shaped and may be appliquéd to the background with primitive stitches. Folk art appliqué often uses fabrics other than 100 percent cotton, including wool, felt, and flannel.

Freezer paper. A household paper with one plastic-coated

side, which sticks to fabric when pressed.

Freezer paper appliqué. A variety of methods that use freezer paper as templates for pattern pieces. A freezer paper shape is pressed onto the fabric, where its plastic coating adheres to it. Freezer paper can be used on top of the fabric as a guide for turning under the fabric edges, or it can be used on the bottom as a stabilizer when stitching the shape. Seam allowance edges are folded back onto the paper and glued, pressed, or basted in place.

Clip here

Freezer paper

Fusible thread. A thread that, when pressed, becomes sticky and fuses together fabrics that touch it. It can be used for "basting" appliqués such as vines, basket handles, or other narrow shapes. Fusible thread is used in the machine needle, with cotton thread in the bobbin.

Fusible web. A paper-backed adhesive product that allows you to permanently affix appliqué pieces directly to the background. Fusible interfacing when used to face appliqués is used in a similar manner.

H

Hawaiian appliqué. Whole-cloth appliqué where the pattern is

made by folding paper into eighths and cutting a design, in a manner similar to children cutting snowflakes. The pattern is traced onto the top layer of fabric, which is then layered onto a background fabric. The design is usually appliquéd with a cutwork technique. See also *Cutwork appliqué*.

L

Light box. A glass- or Plexiglas-topped box containing a bright light that makes tracing appliqué patterns easy. Light boxes are available at quilt shops or art-supply stores, or you can make a temporary one by placing a light beneath a glass or Plexiglas table.

M

Metallic thread. A sparkling, synthetic thread that is wrapped around a polyester core. Use metallic thread with a special machine needle, such as a Metallica or Metalfil, to help prevent the thread from shredding as you sew.

Milliner's needle. A long, thin needle used for hand appliqué. It is longer and more flexible than other hand appliqué needles.

Mock hand appliqué. A type of machine appliqué that uses nylon thread and a narrow zigzag or blind hem stitch to secure the appliqué in place. Because the nylon thread is so fine and nearly invisible, the

result closely resembles invisible hand appliqué.

Mola. Reverse appliqué, where channels or slits are cut in the top layer of fabric to reveal the fabric underneath. Molas are traditionally made by hand by the Cuna people of the San Blas Islands, but they can also be made by machine.

 N

Needle-turn appliqué. Hand appliqué where raw edges are turned under for a very short distance as pieces are sewn to the background. The tip of the needle is used to turn the seam under just before stitching.

Nylon thread. A very fine (.004) thread, used in the sewing machine needle for mock hand appliqué. Available in clear (for light fabrics) or smoke (for dark fabrics), the thread is often difficult to detect in a finished project. Also called monofilament.

 O

Open-toe presser foot. A special sewing machine foot that is cut away in front of the needle to give you a clear view of what you are stitching. It is particularly helpful when using the satin stitch or blanket stitch, where it can be difficult to sew over the bulk of the built-up stitches.

 P

Perle cotton. A twisted thread that produces a rounded appearance on the surface of the fabric. Perle cotton comes in several different thicknesses, including sizes 3, 5, 8, and 12 (the lower the number, the thicker the thread). Perle cotton is commonly used for folk art hand appliqué stitches, including blanket, feather, and running stitches.

Pigma pen. A popular type of permanent marker, available in many colors and pen-tip widths. In hand appliqué, a black or brown pen, size .01, can be used to trace around templates onto the right side of fabric to mark turn-under lines for needle-turn appliqués. The ink is permanent and will not bleed. Brown pens make a slightly softer mark than black pens.

 Q

Quilter's GluTube. A rubber cement product used for basting appliqué shapes to freezer paper templates.

 R

Rayon thread. A synthetic thread that can be used to add sheen to appliqué projects. Rayon thread comes in 30 wt. and 40 wt. Both are suitable for machine appliqué.

Reverse appliqué. Fabric on top is cut away to reveal another fabric underneath. The top fabric is then stitched in place. Reverse appliqué is especially suitable for stitching designs with convex shapes because when stitched in reverse, the top layer, or the concave curve, is what

is stitched. Concave curves have less bulk to smooth into place.

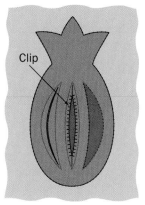

Rotary cutter. A razor-sharp, rolling cutter that resembles a pizza cutter. A rotary cutter is used in conjunction with a special self-healing mat that protects the table surface and an acrylic ruler to cut fabric. For appliqué, it is helpful to have a square ruler (12½ or 15½ inch) for cutting background blocks accurately.

Ruching. Gathering long strips or tubes of fabric with a zigzag running stitch to form three-dimensional flowers, vines, and other designs.

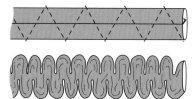

 S

Satin stitch. A narrow zigzag stitch done on the machine to hold the edges of appliqué shapes in place. Stitches are side by side, forming a continuous ribbon of color around the shapes.

Seam allowance. The fabric between a seam and the raw edge. In appliqué, it is the amount of fabric that is turned under when preparing or stitching the appliqué.

Sequin pins. Short (¾-inch) straight pins used to pin-baste appliqué pieces to the background fabric. Because the pins are short, they don't have long tips that can easily catch the thread. However, they are thicker than silk pins, so they create larger holes in the fabric.

Sewing machine needles. The best needles for machine appliqué are embroidery or sharp needles. Choose a size that is large enough to go through the layers (the appliqué, the seam allowance, the background, and the stabilizer) easily, but that isn't so large that it leaves big holes in the fabric. When using metallic thread, a better choice is a special metallic needle, such as Metallica and Metalfil.

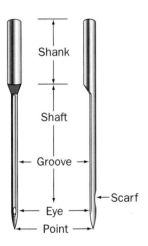

Sharps. Long, thin needles often used for hand appliqué.

Silk pins. Long, very thin straight pins that glide through fabrics easily. These are the finest of straight pins. They leave virtually no holes in the fabric when they are removed.

Silk thread. Preferred by some hand appliquérs, silk thread is very fine and slips through fabric quite easily. It has a higher sheen than cotton thread and is durable since it is a natural fiber.

Spray starch appliqué. Rather than basting them, the edges of shapes are moistened with spray starch, then turned under and pressed to prepare them for appliqué. This method typically uses templates made from Templar, a heat-resistant plastic that can withstand the heat of a moderate iron.

Stabilizer. A material placed between the fabric and the feed dogs during machine appliqué. It helps you achieve more consistent stitching and prevents the background from shifting as you sew. Choose a brand that is easy to tear off when the appliqué is complete.

Straw needles. Used for hand appliqué, these are the longest and most flexible of the hand appliqué needles. Although they tend to bend a bit more easily, some appliquérs prefer them because their length makes them easy to grasp and control. And because they are so thin, they slip easily through the fabric layers.

Templar. Heat-resistant plastic used to make templates.

Template. An exact duplication of a pattern piece. Appliqué templates generally do not include a seam allowance. They can be made of plastic, Templar, freezer paper, or fusible web.

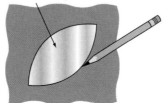

Plastic template

Thimble. A protective device worn on the middle finger of the stitching hand to protect the finger from being pierced by a thin appliqué needle. Thimbles come in many varieties, including metal, leather, plastic, and even suede pads that stick to the finger with adhesive.

W

Water-soluble glue stick. A pastelike substance that comes in a tube form with a screw-on lid. The paste can be applied to the wrong side of an appliqué to adhere it to the background fabric in lieu of basting. The glue will wash away when the quilt is laundered.

Z

Zigzag stitch. The machine stitch used for satin stitching and sometimes for mock hand appliqué. The needle swings from left to right as the stitch advances. The width of the stitch can be modified from very narrow to very wide. Typically, satin stitch is done with a narrow stitch so the thread doesn't detract from the appliqué fabric. See also *Satin stitch*.

Zipper foot. A specialty sewing machine presser foot. In appliqué, it is used for stitching along the side of bias bars to make perfect-width bias tubes. The design of the foot enables you to stitch with the needle right next to the bias bar, without interference.

About the Writers

Karen Kay Buckley has been quilting for 13 years and teaching quilting for 10. She is a popular teacher of both hand and machine appliqué. She has over 200 quilts to her credit, and many have won national and regional awards. Karen has authored two books on quilting.

Mimi Dietrich specializes in teaching Baltimore album–quilt classes using dimensional appliqué techniques. She is actively involved in quilt research with the Smithsonian Institution's National Museum of American History, and she is the author of several quilt books.

Cyndi Hershey has been quilting since 1978 and began teaching quilting in the early 1980s. Her background is in interior design and textiles, and the colors, patterns, and textures of fabric still interest Cyndi the most about quilting. She and her husband, Jim, own The Country Quilt Shop in Montgomeryville, Pennsylvania, where Cyndi teaches as often as possible.

Jane Hill has a master's degree in clothing and textiles, and she began her wearable art designs business, Hillcraft Needle Arts, in 1980. Jane has always been attracted to Molas, the festive, reverse appliqué patterns of the Cuna Indians of Panama, but the amount of handwork was not appealing to her. She traveled to Panama to research for her book *The Electric Mola* and has been teaching her updated, easy-machine version to quilters ever since.

Susan McKelvey is a well-known quiltmaker, teacher, and author. She has written several books, and she teaches quilting throughout the United States. Her quilts have appeared in quilt shows, galleries, and museums. She also designs and distributes quilting books, patterns, and supplies through her company, Wallflower Designs.

Jane Townswick is an editor for Rodale Quilt books. She previously owned a quilt shop and continues to teach advanced appliqué.

Janet Wickell has been quilting for many years, but it became a passion in 1989, when she discovered miniature quilts. She is the sponsor of Minifest, the only national show and seminar devoted to small quilts. For the past several years Janet has been a freelance writer and has recently authored her first quilting book. She teaches quilting and hand-marbling fabric, and she also enjoys herb gardening, photography, and reproducing quilt patterns in stained glass.

Acknowledgments

Quiltmakers

Karen Kay Buckley, Rose Trellis on page 46 and Trip Around the Flower Garden on page 74

Mimi Dietrich, American Beauty Antique on pages 4–5 and 104; appliquéd by students of Mimi Dietrich and quilted by Linda Daigle; Blue Bouquets on page 4, quilted by Joan Glynn Wille; and Traditional Album on page 4

Robbi Joy Eklow, Teapots on page 16

Jane Hall, Mariner's Compass and Princess Feather on page 7 and 84

Laura Heine, Field of Flowers on pages 2–3 and 22

Cyndi Hershey, Wild Roses on page 52 (pattern by Bear Paw Productions), and Lightship Baskets (pattern by Pieces Patchwork Quilting) on page 10

Linda Kranak, The Royal Garden on the cover. (Made from block of the month kit by The Summerhouse Needleworks in Oley, Pennsylvania; pattern by Piece O' Cake Designs)

Sue Linker, Heart's Song on pages 4–5 and on page 112

Maggie Lydic, cutwork appliqué blocks on page 118

Suzanne Nelson, Folk Art Peony on page 62, Sophie's Orchard Star on page 90, and Folk Art Table Cover on page 98 (pattern by Fabric Expressions)

Sue Nickels, Let It Grow on page 38

Jane Townswick, floral appliqué blocks on pages 28, 94, and 118 (pattern for the block on page 28 is by Piece O' Cake Designs), and Blue Clouds on page 78 (pattern published by Jeanna Kimball in her book, *Red and Green Appliqué Quilts*)

Sample Makers

Barbara Eikmeier, Jane Hill, Doris Morelock, Ellen Pahl, Karen Soltys, and Jane Townswick

Fabrics and Supplies

Alaska Dyeworks—hand-dyed fabric
American & Effrid—Mettler thread
Benartex—fabric
Bernina of America—sewing machine
Dream World Enterprises—Sew Steady sewing table
Olfa-O'Lipfa—rotary cutters
Omnigrid—rotary-cutting mats and rulers

INDEX

Quilting Styles

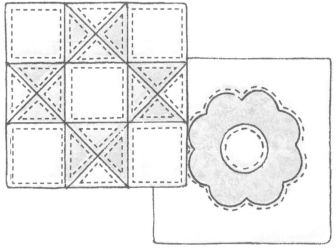

Outline Quilting

Echo Quilting

Single

Double

Crosshatch or Grid Quilting

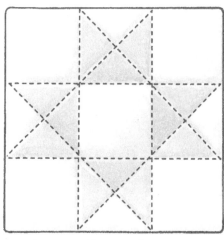

In the Ditch Quilting

Stipple Quilting

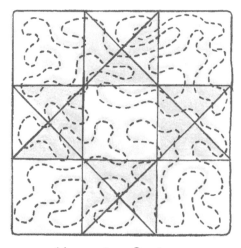

Meander Quilting